Wishing you many happy years of retirement in your backyard paridise.

Jim & Karen Dohrmann

GARDENS
for the SOUL

GARDENS
for the SOUL

SUSTAINABLE & STYLISH
OUTDOOR SPACES

SARA BIRD &
DAN DUCHARS of
The CONTENTed Nest

RYLAND PETERS & SMALL
LONDON • NEW YORK

Senior designer Toni Kay

Editor Sophie Devlin

Senior commissioning editor
  Annabel Morgan

Location research Jess Walton

Head of production Patricia Harrington

Art director Leslie Harrington

Publisher Cindy Richards

First published in 2022 by
Ryland Peters & Small
20–21 Jockey's Fields,
London WC1R 4BW
and
341 East 116th Street
New York, NY 10029

www.rylandpeters.com

Text copyright © The CONTENTed
Nest 2021
Design and photographs copyright
© Ryland Peters & Small 2021
10 9 8 7 6 5 4 3

ISBN 978-1-78879-428-2

A CIP record for this book is
available from the British Library.

Library of Congress CIP data has
been applied for.

Printed and bound in China

CONTENTS

INTRODUCTION

Our gardens are an enchanting sanctuary, somewhere wonderful to share and the perfect place to amble and potter. A captivating and rewarding extension of our homes, they can give so much more pleasure than just plant care by being an inviting, inspiring and intriguing setting in which we feel completely at home.

Our enjoyment of these outdoor rooms is wide-ranging, from entertaining, escape and exercise to individual pastimes. They offer fun, freedom and fresh air right on our own doorstep. The garden can also represent a continuation of our home decor, blurring the boundaries between indoors and out.

More recently, many of us have realized that our gardens offer us an immediate biophilic connection to the natural world with all its health-giving and psyche-nourishing benefits. The opportunity to enhance our wellbeing in a secure outdoor environment could not be more inviting.

Yet it is also in these multi-tasking havens that we can immediately see the cause and effect of our own eco footprint, which affects not just our own backyards but the landscape beyond. The materials we use, the practices we adopt, the amount we consume and the energy we spend can be seen as soon as we step outside. The choices we make as we shape and care for our own green spaces give us the chance to show resourcefulness and seek out sustainable solutions and discover the advantages of working in harmony with nature.

We wanted to make this book in order to share our favourite considered, meaningful and eco-friendly concepts for outdoor spaces. We hope they will inspire you to create memorable settings in your own garden, whether you are working with a petite plot or greater grounds, reinventing an existing garden or starting afresh. We also show you how to devise sheltered, all-weather corners for year-round use. Interwoven throughout are ideas on how to connect with nature while curating personal, soulful garden rooms and experiences. Your garden is not just for now but for years to come.

1
THE ELEMENTS

SURFACES & SCREENS

There are all kinds of borders and boundaries that you can use to frame your space and divide it into distinct areas. Selecting authentic and sustainable materials will give your design a cohesive, individual look.

Garden walls can be precast in concrete or constructed on site using bricks, blocks or flint. Fencing is a fabulous alternative that will age beautifully with the weather. Make sure you source it from an FSC-accredited supplier, if you are buying new, or look for reclaimed fencing as a way to bring in some character. You can choose to emphasize the natural colour and texture of the wood, or paint and seal the fence using eco-friendly paints and preservatives for added interest. Coppiced canes such as hazel or beech can be woven to form handsome hurdles or screens, or even shaped into shelters. Bamboo is fast growing and can be woven into fence panels, making it an incredibly environmentally friendly option.

For a historical edge, try architectural salvage yards for doors, windows and flooring or decorative items such as mirrors, mouldings and other architectural elements. With their patina of age and unknown past lives, these scuffed, chipped and worn pieces are a wonderful opportunity to upcycle a cherished piece of history and bring their own unique presence.

Pergolas, pea canes and plant supports are a valuable addition, too, establishing a framework on which climbers can be trained to form a living screen. Let the plants take hold and they will blend and blur surface edges as they creep up and curl around the underlying structure – the perfect biophilic solution.

STANDOUT STYLE

Colour is a fantastic vehicle to enhance certain moods as well as incorporating favourite shades, such as the zingy yellow of this raised border (opposite) or a calming hue for a more neutral canvas. Pattern also has its place, whether it is a striking tile arrangement or intricate ornamentation in a woven screen. Layering different materials in a variety of finishes is a great way to highlight their complementary characteristics. Quarried stone, painted timber and patinated mirrors (right, from top) bring a sense of individuality. When inheriting materials or reusing what is already installed, consider how to adapt these elements to your own style and give them a lived-in look.

IN THE ZONE

Surfaces can be used to define areas within your outdoor space, allowing you to change the pace from one garden room to another. In this sleek outdoor kitchen and dining area (above), the roof also offers shelter from the elements. Walls, floors and ceilings can be cleverly combined to contain or open up areas, creating a natural flow just as they would inside our homes. Choosing the right texture and finish can make a space feel either transient or inviting, communally on show or a quiet, personal retreat. Nature provides organic opportunities to demarcate our garden rooms; try using plant supports (left) to create living shelters, canopies and partitions that change with the seasons. Equally charming is the way materials age over time, with impressionable patinas and reflective blooms, as seen in this comfortably weathered seating area (opposite).

BETWEEN THE LINES

Instead of solid walls, consider incorporating see-through screening – slatted or open-weave panels that still allow light to pass through while gently dividing and separating. There are a variety of options, such as upcycled fence panels and pallets (opposite). For a more natural approach, try coppiced branches (above left), willow weave (top right) or ornamental planting structures that will lend texture and introduce a living element to an outdoor room.

ALL-WEATHER FABRICS & TEXTILES

Softening, shading, covering and comforting, textiles and linens lend a homely look to our outdoor living rooms. There are ground-to-sky opportunities to bring them into the garden to make tailored and tactile nooks and niches.

Bringing fabric into the garden was once rather impractical, but now there is a plentiful supply of specialist materials designed to be left outside in all weathers. These innovative textiles can be fashioned into outdoor upholstery, soft furnishings, shades and screens. And although most of them are synthetic, many are made from recycled fibres, discarded plastics or even a new breed of plant-based fruit fabrics. Look out for the Greenguard certification, which is awarded to materials that are known to emit low levels of VOCs.

With so many potential uses, these fabrics enable us to bring our indoor style outside into the garden, blurring the boundaries between inside and out. Pattern, colour and texture are just as impactful here as they would be indoors. Consider a pop of colour against a background of green foliage, a soft surface underfoot or an eye-catching graphic print. These ingredients also extend the hours we spend in our gardens. Cushions temper hard seating, rugs make the ground more comfortable and parasols provide welcome shade.

Heritage textiles have their place in the garden, too. Who would be without an eiderdown on a settle or vintage voiles draped from an arbour? If buying new, shop for organic cottons – Global Organic Textile Standard or Organic Content Standard approved – hemps or Oeko-Tex-certified fabrics produced without harmful chemicals.

EASILY SWAYED
Softening hard furniture (bottom left) and adding movement as they waft or blow in the breeze (centre left), fabrics and textiles are a welcome personal touch in the garden. They can line, cover, cushion and shade as needed (opposite), and are effortless to update when the seasons change. You can even create a completely custom look using a patchwork of fabric scraps, as seen on this bench (top left). Weatherproof textiles can be left outside, or indoor styles can be taken outdoors to add a homely feel.

EFFORTLESS ELEGANCE

The right soft furnishings make it easier and more appealing to spend time in the garden. The hessian drapes in this greenhouse (opposite) are an inexpensive and characterful way to shade the interior from harsh sunshine. Washable and weatherproof, cushions and rugs designed for outdoor use (above and right) can be simply hosed down to keep them clean. Robust in all kinds of climates and conditions, they can be left outside all year round and are a practical, long-lasting choice.

FURNITURE & STORAGE

Offering a place to perch at every level, focal points for entertaining or much-needed stow space to display our treasures or stash away essentials, well-chosen furniture will serve its purpose in a stylish and sustainable manner.

Brought into our gardens with practicality in mind, furniture can be much more than just fit for purpose. Comfortable, attractive and well-made seating, tables and storage will invite us to spend more time enjoying our outdoor spaces. These pieces come with a price tag, especially if made to last in all weathers. If purchasing new, it is best to seek out manufacturers who use resources sustainably and keep FSC values at the heart of the making process.

Heritage and heirloom pieces are also welcome in the garden, where they lend character, history and provenance. Carrying less of a carbon footprint than newly produced furniture, they are an eco-friendly option but might need an extra bit of TLC if you want to give them a permanent home outside. Fortunately, there is now an incredible range of eco-friendly paints and stains to refresh and restore wooden furniture, as well as specialist outdoor upholstery fabrics.

As we enjoy our gardens more for different activities, storage is often overlooked. Plan for a mix of built-in and freestanding pieces for flexibility. Shelving, display cases and racks, crates and caddies or hooks and rails offer a chance for off-the-cuff displays, while built-in styles can house more functional accessories. Prime and treat any metal or wooden surfaces to stay the course – or invest in pieces that have been crafted to withstand the elements.

IN THEIR ELEMENT

Whether intended for a certain role or multi-tasking as storage, furniture brings shape and structure to the outdoor room. Choose from sustainable resources if buying a ready-made or bespoke design, or rethink inherited and reclaimed pieces that could serve a new role. Some indoor furniture is fine to take outside, but you may need to treat it using an exterior-grade stain or varnish. Personalize your outdoor furniture with tactile textiles (opposite), or use it to display decorative objects (centre right).

PERFECTLY PLACED

Furniture defines how each area of the garden will be used. It can be a built-in fixture (above), or have certain qualities, such as size, weight or age, that anchor it to a particular spot (opposite). Some pieces are more versatile and can be moved from one space to the next. Furniture can also offer a way to express your style, whether sleek and modern, laidback bohemian, timeless classic or antique elegance. Not everything should be uniform, however – surprising details will stamp individuality onto the garden.

SHELF HELP

Storage can conceal a multitude of oddments or bring treasured objects to the fore. In this dining area (opposite), open shelving is used for rough-hewn logs as well as for potted plants and glowing lanterns. If you are building a bespoke design to fit a particular space or to house objects of a certain size, consider using upcycled materials (above and below left).

VERSATILE STYLES

Freestanding storage can have a laidback look, and may serve more than one purpose. A hose reel cubby (left) or log store (above) could double up as a table, for example. Providing practical hobbying surfaces while storing all manner of things underneath, these everyday arrangements are an efficient use of space as well as being easy on the eye.

LIGHTING & HEATING

Illuminating, atmospheric and inviting, light and heat in our gardens bring a cozy, magical glow, allowing us to linger longer outside and extend not just the hours we spend there but the shifting seasons, too.

There is something wonderfully enticing about twinkling lights and flickering flames – they catch the eye, draw us near and bring a sense of contentment wherever they are seen. Rather remarkably, what could be just a practical element can also soothe and enrich the dwindling and cooler hours spent outdoors.

There is now a vast array of both decorative and functional lighting choices for the garden, including eco-friendly solar-powered options. You can showcase features with spotlights, define and delineate with posts and path markers, brighten gathering spaces with hanging lanterns and lamps or add charm and fascination with garlands of fairy lights. And then there is the great appeal of candles and torches.

Providing a feel-good flicker, they add life, colour and even scent to an outdoor setting. You can choose a cleaner and more sustainable flame by going for high-quality, ethically produced natural wax and oil-based candles instead of paraffin wax, which is derived from fossil fuels.

The seasonal sway of the weather means keeping cozy outside has its challenges, and extra clothing and woollen blankets can only do so much. Introducing a fireside element is an obvious choice, bringing a campfire feel to our gardens and enticing us to gather round a log or biofuel firepit or a charming chiminea. Bringing the added benefit of easy cookouts, these outdoor fireplaces and stoves warm the air while we enjoy their inviting glow.

LIGHT-BULB MOMENTS

When considering how to illuminate your garden, it is always best to make a plan. Consider where you will need task lighting, what the desired atmosphere is for each area and any other requirements. Finish with the starry-eyed details from joyous festoons to dreamy lanterns and overhead spots (top left). Safely wire each light to the nearest power point using outdoor plugs, making sure that all wires have watertight coverings. Solar-powered lights are a great renewable alternative. Candles and tealights (centre left and opposite) are a great way to bring atmosphere to your garden.

SET THE SCENE

Coming into its own when the sun sets, lighting can make an immediate impression and offers the chance to engage with the garden in a different ambience. From party-perfect illumination for an atmosphere of feel-good frivolity when entertaining (above) to a soulful glow suitable for romance, indulgence or a sense of escapism (opposite), there are brilliantly bright and quietly incandescent options to be explored.

STOKE THE FLAMES

A step up from a traditional bonfire, outdoor heating is now widely available in more sophisticated forms. Purpose-built furnaces and firepits engage, warm and delight, and are a joy to be around. Other possibilities include a cookery station with griddles and racks for open-air grilling, or in-the-round biofuel burners to heat a communal area or to encourage late-night lounging. If you are a keen upcycler, think outside the box – imaginative solutions include this beer keg stove (opposite), which was built by a family who like to spend time together cozying up and toasting marshmallows over the flames.

GLOW GIVERS

A classic firepit is a simple style that invites everyone to gather round like moths to a flame, but there are plenty of garden-warming options depending on your personal style and how you like to use your outside space. Here we have an olde-worlde chiminea (above) and a sleek, modern outdoor wood burner (right).

ON DISPLAY

A great way to express our individuality, presenting our personally collected objects is a chance to create talking points, share our passions, reveal our personalities and bring an element of fun to all who enjoy our gardens.

With our outdoor spaces now being an extension of our homes and ourselves, who we are can be celebrated outside, too. What better way to do this than to create spaces for our favourite things as souvenirs from where we have been or what we have experienced? Their presence reveals what is unique about us and brings character by the bucketload.

Objects lend their own qualities to a space with their colour, shape, texture and style. They can work together as a collection based on a particular theme or stand out on their own. Favourite items that are used on a daily basis have a unique charm and deserve to be showcased, while ornamental treasures will always grab attention. Either way, they are sure to add spirit to an empty corner or spark conversation in a lulled moment. Even the most modest pot or jar can be enjoyed for all to see.

Part of the fun is deciding what to display and how to arrange it. This can be done according to the function of the object, such as a grouping of tools or utensils, or you may prefer an artful arrangement of randomly gathered gizmos. Artisan and vintage pieces bring a sense of authenticity to any collection as well as fascinating stories about their origins. If more delicate items need protection from the elements, think about staging them in sealed but see-through containers. Glazed cabinets, salvaged windowpanes, cloches and jars are a weatherproof way to to show off these treasured finds, helping you bring a bit of the indoors out.

SHOW AND TELL

Reinventing and reusing the reclaimed enables us to create unique display areas and bring warmth and character to the garden. Here, a wooden fruit crate has been transformed into a whimsical wall-hung planter (opposite), and a bucket makes a simple hanging basket in which to pot up pretty flowers (centre right). Shapely decorative elements integrated into a green space, such as ornamental stakes (top right), are sure to spark conversation. You could also create an arrangement of textured plant pots and vases (bottom right), or anything else that makes you smile.

TIMEWORN TREASURES

Beauty can be found in the quotidian and average, even in the simplest utensils that we use on a daily basis. In these pared-back sheds and summer houses, curated displays bring together gardening tools, found objects and decorative items such as lanterns and vases. Plentiful pots, collected cast-offs and groupings of similar things have gravitas and impact, and one-off statement pieces can be used to transform the unremarkable into the extraordinary.

PLANT POWER

The advantage of styling a garden room is the ability to enjoy greenery all year round in various displays. We can gather clusters of favourite plants or move them around to refresh different areas. They present an instant and direct way to engage with the natural world, and there is endless enjoyment to be found in tending specimens and keeping blooms at their best. Plants and flowers add mood-boosting colour and texture to an outdoor seating area (opposite). You can even group scented varieties together to offer a curated aromatic experience just like creating a perfume. Planters in all shapes and sizes can be arranged on surfaces, shelving, wall-mounted hangers and on the floor. Miniature pots (above and right) are great way to introduce children to gardening. Projects to capture their attention might involve sowing seeds or picking their first harvest.

CREATING A SENSE OF WELLBEING

Harnessing the mindful. health-giving benefits of outdoor living is the secret to creating a garden for the soul. Observing the changing seasons and interacting with nature are truly satisfying, life-enhancing experiences.

Being in our gardens is not just about the toil of the soil. Spending time outside offers us the chance to find our feet and ourselves, relax in our surroundings, disconnect, slow down and top up on needed me (and us) time. A garden should be a mood-enhancing setting in order to rebalance our wellbeing and delight all our senses with colour, texture, scent and sound. Incorporate rippling and rustling materials to brush against, candles to flicker and fragrance, water flow and wind chimes for soothing sound and fluttering fringes and swaying lanterns for enchanting movements.

How we inhabit and interact with our gardens has the potential to greatly enhance the calming effects of spending time outdoors. Savouring the seasons with cooking and eating, picking and preserving or simply pottering and playing will all help you connect with the natural world. Ideally, your outdoor space should be easily accessible when the weather allows – even when you are inside the house, keep doors and windows open so that you spend as much time engaging with the garden as possible.

Encouraging and supporting the wildlife in your garden brings further feel-good moments that will help you interact more with nature and the wider world. Install ponds, houses and feeding stations for shelter, food and rest. Choosing not to brush away every cobweb, watching mini beasts active and about their business or listening to birdsong makes us pause and be still for a moment.

CREATURE COMFORTS

Many of us share our outside spaces with our pets, such as these chickens (bottom left), and with wild visitors who give us the scope to care for them. How we invite them in can benefit our wellbeing, too. We can introduce colour and scent to attract insects, grow certain varieties of flowers for particular bees and butterflies, provide food for birds (opposite) and introduce shelter, shade and a hide for all (top left).

TAP INTO WELLNESS

Introducing a water feature into a garden offers the joy of sound and motion. Be it a pond, stream, fountain or bird bath (opposite top left and right), it extends the chance to engage with a proven mood enhancer. Water features also invite us to stop and watch (below), observing and listening to the waves and ripples or noticing the wildlife attracted to them. It opens a window of stillness.

HOME-GROWN DELIGHTS

From plot to plate, growing something to eat from scratch brings much pleasure (opposite bottom right). Through the process of caring and tending, the discovery of new growth, the pride taken in the pulling up or picking to the final taste, the cycle of producing a home-grown harvest can be enjoyed by all ages. It also brings us closer to our fellow enthusiasts, with whom we can bond over shared experiences or exchange advice.

NATURAL CONNECTIONS

Outdoor living can inspire such a sense of satisfaction and fulfilment by bringing the benefits of biophilia to our doorsteps. Our interactions with nature support our mental wellbeing as much as our physical health, helping us to switch off and slow down. To enjoy your garden to the fullest, create places to engage in green pastimes and hobbies, marvel at the natural world in quiet corners and make time to delight in all the sights, sounds and scents around you.

2
THE GARDENS

GREAT ESCAPERS

SECRET *sanctuary*

When Julie Aldridge first viewed the cottage that would become her home, she felt drawn to the overgrown garden, which she found wonderfully romantic. Now, after a major renovation project, she loves to escape outdoors after a busy day and lose herself among the planting.

As you step into Julie Aldridge's garden, the wider world seems to slow down. Behind her picturesque cottage, she has created a serene collection of secluded outdoor spaces away from the hustle and bustle of everyday life. Dotted around the periphery are the most perfect of private pockets, each designed in a cohesive contemporary cottage style with a wealth of handmade details and inspiring ideas.

The garden presented an intriguing opportunity to unearth and untangle overgrown and forgotten areas. An existing pond garden was past its best, outbuildings requiring some

LEFT & ABOVE
An inherited vine drapes around a pergola, shading an upcycled dining table and vintage seating in the perfect breakfast spot just outside the house. Lanterns and festoon lights make this a space to enjoy at all hours whatever the time of year.

OPPOSITE
Seats in a variety of heights and styles are on offer in this casual outdoor sitting room. The rug, pouffes, garden bench and upholstered sofa reflect the monochromatic scheme, with a cohesive mix of geometric patterns. It is an inviting place to sit and relax.

TLC and feature walling hidden from view. The space was in need of a gentle helping hand.

Over time, Julie has given this garden a new sense of purpose. She considered how it could be used with the aim of being able to spend every free hour outside. Julie first observed the light to see where the best suntraps and shaded areas might be. She then worked with nature to help the garden flourish. Crops and flowers for cutting were helped to thrive, and the existing structures and inherited shrubs carefully examined to decide what should be encouraged, revamped and rescued.

ABOVE & LEFT

An original pantile-roofed outbuilding has been updated indoors and out to make a fully functioning potting shed. Whitewashed boards bring a fresh feel to the interior, where garden equipment, plants and decorative objects are displayed on open shelving created from wooden pallets. The tonal scheme on the inside is carried through to the outside with a practical and pretty rug. The exterior walls feature a contemporary and smart black finish. This was achieved using a wood stain from Protek, which makes eco-friendly protective coatings for outdoor surfaces in a range of colours.

PAGE 51
One of Julie's favourite garden projects was the greenhouse. Saved from the scrapheap, this year-round room features simple hessian drapes, wooden flooring and adaptable furniture. The rustic textures of these reclaimed and recycled materials are well suited to the garden environment. The overhead lighting is magical when the evenings draw in.

Particularly rewarding was the chance to update the garden buildings with reclaimed materials and furniture. A potting shed was reborn from a cluttered and down-at-heel cabin. Blighted boards on the walls were replaced with wooden cladding and linoleum was laid on the floor to make it easy to keep clean. An existing wooden bench was sanded down and practical shelving was made from upcycled delivery crates. Further storage is provided by a beautiful old dresser/hutch, an antique-shop find that now houses a collection of vases and garden pots.

The greenhouse was another rescue project. Once a local gardener had fixed the broken panes, a few low-cost changes made a big difference. First, Julie painted the framework with a black eco-friendly wood stain to give it a contemporary look. Inside, she added simple floorboards, hessian drapes, a repurposed table and festoon lights. Now the space beckons to be used at all hours, for all manner of purposes.

OPPOSITE
Snug and sociable, this corner sofa occupies a once-hidden area of the garden next to a beautiful flint wall. The wall's natural texture is reflected in Julie's choice of furniture from the Danish brand Muubs, which combines raw stone with robust metalwork in its contemporary designs. Julie applied masonry paint to the floor, ensuring that it will weather to perfection with age and use.

ABOVE
Once the hard landscaping and furniture were in place, Julie started to bring in soft furnishings and homewares to establish a comfortable atmosphere. Natural linens lend an effortless look to this low-key outdoor dining room, in which simple Scandi-inspired pieces instil a classic, timeless feel. Wall lanterns and festoon lights allow the space to be used late into the night.

The summer house, which had been cherished by the previous owners, was also saved and strengthened with side wall supports. Over the years, repainting work on both inside and out, hessian drapes, new furniture and lights have kept it looking fresh. Overlooking the pond, it offers a chance to watch the wildlife or to wind down and enjoy the reflection of the light on the surface of the water.

The garden is very much a private place, but Julie has created a summery suntrap that is ideal for cooking, dining and socializing when she has guests. In this formerly overgrown area, which she has cleared of cobwebs, clutter and a run-down shed, masonry paint has been utilized to make a beautiful floor on a budget. Fruit beds and trees offer plot-to-plate inspiration, and bamboo and grasses have been combined with stylish shading. The small outdoor kitchen can accommodate slow-roast Sundays or quick-fire pizza parties.

Every garden vista has been designed to promote a peaceful and soothing experience. A measured tonal mix of white and green planting blends with monochromatic furnishings. Texture can be found in the worn vintage materials, which lend a comforting and informal touch.

The garden offers mood-boosting benefits, too. Well-considered lighting creates an enchanting atmosphere at dawn and dusk, seating areas are surrounded by beautiful scented herbs and there are plenty of opportunities to observe and engage with the local wildlife. There is a simple satisfaction in being able to disconnect on a daily basis within one of its many secluded spots. This is a place to rebalance and restore.

RIGHT
The perfect recipe for an outdoor kitchen space features plenty of storage, as well as space for food preparation and cooking. Julie's kitchen is made of cast concrete and birch ply, and was finished with an exterior paint and stain from Protek. The work surface has been designed to fit around her outdoor grill and stove, and there is room for an occasional pizza oven, too.

RIGHT

An inherited pond is now home to a new generation of wildlife. As well as being a place where flora and fauna can thrive, the area is the perfect spot to unwind while engaging with nature at close range.

FAR RIGHT

The linoleum floor of the summer house was a chance to design some bespoke detailing. Taking inspiration from her favourite tile patterns, Julie had this bold monochrome motif printed to order. Linoleum's hardwearing nature makes it an excellent flooring solution for an outdoor structure.

LEFT, ABOVE & OPPOSITE

The styling and revamping of the old, existing summer house is one of the garden's success stories. Making good the wall panelling, updating the interior and exterior paint and covering unsightly roofing structures with hessian drapes have brought a contemporary country feel. The building now has many uses and is best seen and occupied at sunset when the lighting is at its most beautiful.

URBAN *oasis*

Designer Abigail Ahern's sun-dappled secret city garden is the most beautiful of green spaces just waiting to be discovered. Exquisitely nurtured and refined over time, this hidden haven shelters behind inner boundary walls and under handsome tree canopies. It is a striking and scenic urban landscape for friends and family to delight in.

By Abigail's own admission, the garden is very different from its earliest incarnation, when she introduced quieter and subtler planting and terrain. Over time, the pebble and grass display fell short of her individual style, but today it is a different story. The original design has made way for a wilder, grander and suitably more statuesque collection of mature trees and green rooms with handsome sculptural furniture sited among the boughs and branches.

Conscientiously cared for, the garden's gradual transformation was influenced by Abigail's many travels, from lush tropics to mountainous peaks. The engaging greenery

OPPOSITE
A double-height extension backs out onto the garden, creating a wonderful blurred threshold area with a rough-hewn bench just outside the door. Tall trees are reflected in the exterior glazed walls.

ABOVE AND RIGHT
Particular attention has been made to external lighting to ensure the garden has year-round appeal. Abigail took a bespoke approach, combining practical pendants with wall-mounted installations and charming festoon lights.

LEFT
There are abundant storage and display areas throughout the garden. These include a number of tables where Abigail likes to place some of her favourite grasses and plants in the vessels that she sells in her own store. To one side, a wood store is kept fully stocked for the outdoor fireplace and firepit. And in the kitchen area, a useful top shelf is kept clear for food preparation.

RIGHT
Abigail has incorporated many homewares into the garden so that it feels more like an indoor space. Walls are dressed with decorative displays, a chandelier hangs from a tree canopy 'ceiling' and the furniture, including a waxed paper-covered sofa and a glossy polished table, is pleasingly textured.

she encountered abroad has found its path back to her own outdoor space, where swaying bamboo mingles with feathery ferns and trailing ivy. It is an incredibly restorative and soothing garden to spend time in.

And it is this uplifting, moving and sensory aspect that is most appreciated by Abigail and all who have the chance to experience it in this secret, soulful setting. The rustling of foliage resonates around the garden, amplified by the closed-in nature of the planting, while favourite scented herbs and flowers fill the air with clarifying and cleansing fragrance. It is a positive and welcoming space in which life's stresses and concerns ebb away, and it is tempting to tune out and lose oneself more than just once in a while. Abigail feels a close connection with the garden even when she is not in it, such is the feeling of heightened perception it offers. Just looking out from the windows can help her reconnect to this outer biosphere.

Being in this environment has the added advantage of stimulating Abigail's creativity. Surrounding oneself with pattern, colour, light, texture and form in daily life can inspire the imagination, ingenuity and vision. Essential attributes for anyone working in the design industry, these energizing qualities influence our thought processes with such subtle nuance that they sometimes go unnoticed but benefit the mind and balance the spirit.

Abigail's design background also plays a role in her confident use of colour. The palette of greenery in the garden ranges from softly

LEFT
For reasons of practicality, Abigail has installed Millboard wood-effect composite decking, a low-maintenance choice that needs no preservatives and does not warp or fade.

BELOW
An inviting place to gather around when socializing, this firepit offers warmth and light on cool evenings. Its small size means it can be moved to wherever it is needed.

This concrete table has a variety of potential uses. Not just for dining, it also serves as an extra breakout space for work or play. It has a sociable circular shape and is teamed with a mix of dining and easy chairs depending on who is sitting where. Lighting is provided in the form of draped festoons overhead.

LEFT
This cabin was found via Ebay and came at an unbelievably low price. With its exterior painted black, it is a handsome addition to Abigail's garden. The cabin has found a new lease of life here, serving as a charmingly bijou studio and shelter, and as a play space for her sister's children when they visit.

BELOW LEFT
A pinboard is placed inside the cabin, directly opposite the entrance so that it has a close connection to the natural world outside. A place to gather favourite things, to collect ideas and inspiration and to place everyday ephemera, it is a wonderful way to share thoughts and dreams.

OPPOSITE
Used as an office space where Abigail can work on her designs, the cabin is a fully functioning garden room with heat, light and electricity, making it a viable alternative to working indoors. The window above the desk offers a view straight onto the garden. A change being as good as a rest, working surrounded by plants can feed a creative mind.

bleached foreground leaves to deeper black-greens in the shadows. These shades are mirrored in her choice of furniture and fixtures. Materials, too, have been chosen with conviction: smooth all-weather synthetics, waxed paper, cast concrete and tumbled timber.

The garden has been designed to be used all year round with many internal fittings and fixtures being installed outside. Heating and lighting have been integrated to cater for the seasons, with a cozy fireplace and sociable firepit dressed with chandeliers, pendants and underplant lamps, festoon and string lights and a host of candles and lanterns. A cabin towards the rear acts as a bijou outdoor studio for Abigail and as a place where her sister's children enjoy playing hide and seek. There is also ample seating dotted around. Shapely in style, it is designed for leisurely reclining rather than just quick perching. The garden is a great outdoor entertaining space, with areas offering many places to hide or hole up in for all ages.

Not just family and friends but wildlife is welcome here, too. Birds and mini beasts visiting the garden discover a welcome urban refuge among the ample greenery, much to the excitement of Mungo and Myrtle, Abigail's pet dogs. Observing the rhythms of nature has resulted in a harmonious and biodiverse habitat in this garden, in spite of its city setting.

PASTURES *new*

When she inherited a former market garden and a paddock of horses, Linda Kilburn dreamed of creating her own lake. Over the past 22 years, she has achieved her wish in the form of a nature-inspired lagoon.

An early adopter of sustainable design, Linda has used natural and reclaimed materials to establish different areas in the space. The desire for a lake stemmed from wanting a waterside retreat where she could escape from the stresses of work and find a sense of calm.

Part of the field was dug out to create the lake, into which water from the existing beck now filters before being streamed back out again. The whole system works in harmony with nature and supports the environment.

THIS PAGE & BELOW LEFT
The covered pool house is an enclosed social space designed for relaxation and entertaining. Made from reclaimed beams and stone, it recreates the feel of Mediterranean living and can be enjoyed all year round thanks to the walls and roof that shelter the space from the weather. Snug sofas line the walls on either side of the fireplace, around the centrally located dining table.

An added surprise on reaching the lake is the new boat house, which was built from reclaimed and sustainable materials including green oak beams and grilles rescued from a salvage yard. Approached via a boardwalk, the building is obscured from view by bulrushes, which create the impression of having stumbled upon a secret hideout.

Elsewhere in the garden, Linda has continued this theme of unexpected encounters to heighten the experience of engaging with the outdoor space. Rather than terracing the slope down to the lake, she envisioned an amphitheatre where the family can hold special events by the water for every occasion. Over the years, it has

hosted bands, fireworks and performances marking birthdays, seasonal celebrations and charity fundraisers.

Closer to the main house, a Mediterranean-style swimming pool area transports guests to warmer climes with fragrant plants and bountiful fruit trees. The adjacent pool house was built from reclaimed timbers and stone, and offers protection from the elements. Both were designed with escape in mind. The building, which is used for dining and entertaining, has its own fireplace and a hot tub installed under glass to keep in the warmth.

ABOVE RIGHT

There are many salvaged and sustainable items used in the garden, from rehomed flooring and roof tiles to old farming tools. Timeworn, rusted finishes are welcome, bringing a grounding sense of heritage and authenticity, and establishing a link to the past.

RIGHT

The design of the pool house includes a window in the thick stone wall at the rear. The aperture, which is similar to those in the main house, brings the garden into the space. A wood stain has been used on the window frame to mirror the texture and colour of the green oak beams.

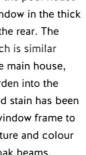

ABOVE

An expansive terrace surrounds the pool and is a natural suntrap, in keeping with the Mediterranean-inspired planting. The flowers and foliage temper the hard stone paving and have been chosen to echo those found in southern Europe. A pair of poolside loungers are softened by cushions in aqua and cerulean hues picked up from the enticing waters nearby.

Having lived her early life as a farmer's daughter, Linda has always felt a strong connection with nature. Inheriting the four-and-a-half-acre plot was a welcome opportunity to revisit her happy childhood, which was spent mostly outdoors. She has introduced beloved plants that she associates with this period of her life: the lake is surrounded by bulrushes, which she remembers bringing home to her mother from nearby ponds when she was young. Nowadays, Linda enjoys taking leisurely woodland walks and observing the wildlife. Just a short walk from the lake house, the stream is a place to stop and watch kingfishers or follow the trout in the water. Finding a moment for this soothing ritual never fails to clear her mind and lift her spirits.

Linda delights in sharing this personal garden with her family and friends. Everyone who visits feels the benefit of engaging with this evocative setting. For herself and her loved ones, this is a place for life's celebrations, where they can share memories and create new ones for the next generation.

ABOVE & OPPOSITE

The lake was one of the first projects embarked on by Linda, who wanted to create a waterside hideaway. For this reason, it was sited farthest from the house, where conveniently there was already a local beck. The lake draws its water from this sustainable source. Cooling rushes and grasses on the banks provide welcome shade, as well as an enticing swishing sound as they rustle and sway in the breeze. The wooden boat house is approached via a winding jetty and is partially screened by wetland planting. The deck in front of the building is a sunny, secluded spot from which to observe and be charmed by the wildlife in and around the water.

RUSTIC *retreat*

Inspired by memories of relaxing holiday hideaways and escapes to sun-soaked Mediterranean islands, Laura and Mark Stubbs' summery sanctuary offers a soulful place for friends and family to gather, relax and unwind just outside their countryside home.

On a hillside with views into the woodlands and lush grasses, the pair have constructed a beautiful cabin that brings a Balearic vibe to their back garden. The structure came about almost by accident after they took on the refurbishment of a neglected former

mill, where they now live, and the adjacent one-acre plot, which was something of a wilderness. The house is at the bottom of a gentle slope and there were earthworks butting up to the property, which Laura and Mark cleared to create a patio.

ABOVE & OPPOSITE

A fantastic place to hang out and chill, the cabin is furnished with lots of relaxing holiday-inspired seating for intimate parties or gatherings of Laura's wider circle. The expansive banquette bench can accommodate a large number of guests, making it a very sociable space. A hammock suspended from the ceiling serves as a comfortable easy chair for restful swaying.

The five-year renovation project led to the build-up of an enormous pile of soil, building materials and other debris. Wanting to avoid adding to landfill, the couple kept the heap and over the years nature took over and enveloped the area, giving it a new character. Wildlife and meadow and woodland flowers now thrive on the hillside, which has been utterly transformed.

It was at this point that Laura and Mark began to make plans for a laidback staycation lodge. They wanted to rekindle memories of their travels in the Mediterranean, where relaxation was a priority and and every possible moment was spent outside.

The cabin was built using leftover materials from the main house. Cinder blocks were laid, then rendered with a soft mottled finish, and roof tiles rescued and fitted. Storm-felled trees from their garden were stripped of their bark by hand and turned into wooden beams. The wood grain has aged beautifully over time and lends a tactile texture to the structure.

The interior has a natural look, with raw surfaces and a neutral palette of slubby cottons, relaxed linens and grass-based weaves. Items sourced from bazaars and independent shops are abundant. Layered cushions soften a bank of timber-topped built-in seating. The reed-covered ceiling brings a darker tone to the predominantly pale scheme for a cozy feel.

OPPOSITE
Despite having two open sides, the building feels snug and cozy due to its clever combination of materials. The rendered walls have a sculptural feel, reeds line the ceiling and the wooden beams establish a link to the local terrain. A macramé wall hanging and woven fabrics add further texture.

RIGHT
Laura has softened the hard concrete floor with a number of rugs and throws that catch the sunlight beautifully.

BELOW
There are a few concessions to modern living in the design of the cabin, one of which is electricity. Candles create ambience, but there are some electric lights, too. A built-in cupboard at one end of the banquette houses a refrigerator.

OPPOSITE TOP LEFT

Hanging planters are the perfect way to introduce a variety of greenery. Easy to change with the seasons, they allow you to display plants at any height.

OPPOSITE TOP RIGHT

A wicker pendant lends a sculptural look to the ceiling and is protected from the elements. This overhead light was a practical choice that has allowed Laura and Mark to realize their dream of being able to spend evenings in the open air.

OPPOSITE BOTTOM LEFT

Inspired by her travels abroad, Laura has used a collection of her favourite baskets to decorate the walls. Souvenirs and finds make for an individual display and evoke happy memories of faraway places.

OPPOSITE BOTTOM RIGHT

The interior styling really brings that casual, laidback charm. Laura chose crumpled linens and relaxed weaves with a rumpled and scrunched feel that call to be touched and lounged on.

RIGHT

Laura has used a rope-ladder-style shelf to display candles and finds. This one is easy to recreate using salvaged wood. Simply saw three planks to the right size and drill holes in the corners. Then thread rope through the holes, knotting on the underside of each plank to secure.

Power is supplied to the cabin from the nearby house, so there is electric lighting for night-time use. The building even has its own refrigerator, which is enclosed within a built-in cupboard with a wooden door.

The cabin now brings back fond memories of family holidays in sunnier climes, and its open-sided design promotes engagement with the former wilderness that surrounds it. It is a peaceful hideaway where Laura and her family can get back in touch with the wider world. Spending time there is always a tranquil, relaxing experience, aided by the proven wellbeing benefits of being immersed in nature. A place to tune out and wind down, it gives the couple and family an ideal space in which to spend quality time together.

GARDEN PARTIERS

NATURAL *flow*

From its organic origins to its ongoing evolution, a relaxed vibe fills this soulful garden space, where its owners Kate and Simon Revere can break away from the everyday and enjoy time with their family.

RIGHT
Homewares are taken inside and out as needed, and Kate's love of plants is evident from her collected assortment of pots and planters. These are used to fill in empty spaces or introduce colour and texture if a particular spot is looking too plain. The moveable display changes with the seasons, allowing the family to refresh their garden as often as they like.

OPPOSITE
A blend of vintage and contemporary styles makes for a colourful scheme in the garden. Kate devised a bold yellow paint that reminds her of a recent trip to Marrakech. The sofa is covered with brightly patterned cloths and cushions from her shop, Revere the Residence. The sight of a disco ball popping up in the border planters is enough to make anyone smile.

Colourful and eclectic, Kate and Simon Revere's garden is a medley of spontaneous and free-flowing features in the most natural of settings. The diverse outdoor space came together in a random manner with no particular plan other than to be a space that their young family could share.

Having spent time abroad, Kate and Simon were keen to settle when they returned to the UK. Despite being a tangle of weeds, the inherited garden they took on was the opportune place to put down some roots. The fallen trees and overgrown nettles and ivy were all removed, leaving just the silver birch, which they kept for its beauty, as well as to provide shade and screening. The no-plan plan settled harmoniously into place as the seasons went by. Relying on instinct and imagination over illustrations, Kate and Simon embraced accidental discoveries and casually collected items – a tile here and a piece of furniture there. Gradually, four distinct garden zones began to emerge within the original space.

ABOVE
Fun elements can be found around every corner of this surprising garden. Kate's more-is-more approach is inspired by fashion, interiors and high days and holidays. A pair of flamingos, found in a vintage shop, take pride of place.

Kate and Simon knew they wanted a seating space near the back door, so this area was dug out to create an outdoor living and dining room. Patterned floor tiles establish a link back to the kitchen. The surrounding fence is made from western red cedar, one of the most sustainable and eco-friendly construction materials. The raised borders, built using painted and rendered cinder blocks, were initially planned to be lower, but their design was revised so as not to waste any excess soil. Their bold yellow hue, inspired by a trip to Marrakech and replacing the original grey paint, brings a holiday ambience to what is now called the Ibiza Zone. Potted tree ferns, bamboo and banana plants add a jungle feel and can be moved around like furniture. Kate's future plans for this area include a pergola to partially shade the dining area, while the sofa will remain uncovered for daytime sun worshipping and evening stargazing.

Next up is the Vintage Garden, screened by a row of cordyline palms. A set of heavy antique benches bought in Paris dictated the gravel flooring, as mowing around them would have been difficult. Bordered by old railway sleepers/railroad ties and featuring plants from Kate and Simon's childhood homes, this area has great sentimental value. It also gets the first sunshine of the day and

ABOVE
Kate has confidently combined contemporary and vintage metal furniture in the dining area. The sleek, minimal benches can be tucked neatly away under the matching table, while an old filigree chair is a handsome addition that contrasts without clashing. Both designs echo the monochrome palette of the tiled flooring, with tableware and accessories from Kate's store introducing pops of colour.

OPPOSITE
A vibrant jungle atmosphere is at the heart of the lower-level seating area, thanks to tall tree ferns and palms in oversized planters and bespoke large raised beds. With plenty of soil, shelter and support, these tropical plants are able to care for themselves and save on water while providing a lush tree canopy for the family to sit under. The heavy vegetation is also used to screen off the rest of the garden, a trick Kate has adopted to define each of the different zones and allow them to flourish and thrive independently.

FAR LEFT
This contemporary sculpture is made from beautifully rusted metal bands.

LEFT
Borders planted with Kate's favourite ferns are edged with reclaimed railway sleepers/railroad ties.

OPPOSITE & BELOW
Brocante benches discovered in Paris give the Vintage Garden its name and feel. Dressed with some of Kate's cushions, they add a little French flair to this elegant setting.

is where the family gathers in the morning under the boughs of the silver birch to drink tea and plan the day ahead.

The go-with-the-flow approach fell into place in the flower beds, too, which were installed opposite the benches. The original idea was to plant them with only white blooms, but other colours soon found a home and were welcomed as a beautiful addition to the planting scheme. More recently, a pod-like structure has landed in the upper garden and serves a dual purpose as home office and creative space.

Beyond this lies the Secret Garden. The main grassed area on this plot development is still in its infancy, but for now a shed made from leftover floorboards has been put up and there are raised beds made from recycled tanks. The main flowers are roses, which fill the air with the most beautiful scent.

In keeping with the organic approach, the family's vegetable patch found its place at the front of the house. It is a real conversation starter where freshly harvested produce and neighbourly catch-ups are easily shared.

PARTY *central*

Theresa Gromski has brought a beautifully bohemian vibe to her intentionally created outer 'indoor' space, which she designed as a setting where she could play host to family and friends as well as a place for pottering and pastimes. It is truly a garden for all occasions.

The prospect of inheriting what was a long, grassy space gave Theresa the momentum to create an interesting and personal outdoor setting for all to enjoy. Eclectic, eco-focused and influenced by her travels, her garden is filled with joyful and sustainable ideas for year-round entertaining. In this sociable space, a series of outdoor living rooms are linked together along a generous length of hedged lawn, with each zone playing a different role.

LEFT & RIGHT
The living area has been designed to entice visitors outside. Screened by hedges and with many homely touches to soften the hard landscaping, there are comforts to enjoy in every corner. A mix of different materials ensures there are plenty of textures to take in and it is this layering that lends an indoor mood to the outdoor space. The rugs, throws, mirrors, collected pots and planters and even the draped lighting dress the hedges and take the edge off the feeling of being outside.

First up and directly off from the kitchen is a snug and cozy outdoor living room intended to be used as much as its indoor counterpart. To make this possible, Theresa has taken many home comforts outside. There are rugs on the floor to soften and warm hard paving stones. Cushions, seat pads and bolsters have been layered on sofas and chairs. The styling of the setting positively encourages relaxing and lazing with its generously sized furniture, too. There is even a fireside area with a chiminea and a feature mirror to the side. A confident use of pattern and Theresa's signature tonal colour scheme clearly mark the way for this outdoor room to be used and appreciated.

ABOVE & LEFT
Theresa has used potted plants for natural screening to the side of the seating area. Like window netting or drapes, the fronds and ferns soften harsh lighting and provide shade from the wind and weather. A chance to connect with nature within arm's reach, they can be moved around to where they are needed.

OPPOSITE
A handmade sofa fills the outdoor living space. Created from pressure-treated scaffolding boards, it is generously proportioned and allows all the family to sit down together. Summer dressing includes plenty of cushions and throws; blankets are added during the winter months for longer and cozier lingering.

LEFT

There is much use of sustainable materials throughout, including rattan for furniture. Much quicker to grow than trees and with each vine producing yards of material, rattan is harvested by hand and replanted in quick succession. As the vines rely on trees to grow, rattan production also encourages forest retention.

BELOW LEFT

Theresa has chosen adaptable furniture for much of the outdoor space. Here, a bench acts as a table when it is not in use and is a handy place for an assortment of pots and planters. A versatile alternative to shelving, benches offer a space to display personal collections of objects but can easily be cleared if extra seating is required.

BELOW

Like many gardens, Theresa's has a large lawn where her growing family can play. At other times, a bench can easily be installed for conversation and downtime. It also acts as an unintrusive low-level temporary structure that breaks up the large expanse of green space without obscuring the views beyond, which would be hidden by something taller.

The family are keen upcyclers, as the furniture in the living space attests. The sofa is made from reclaimed scaffolding boards and is set on castors, making this a moveable and practical design that can make way for more people if needed. More of the boards are used as wooden decks, which butt up to the pavers to extend the lounging space. All the boards have been left in their original tanalized finish; this eco-friendly pressure treatment preserves wood for many years. A coffee table and herb planter, meanwhile, have been made from upcycled wooden pallets. These have been finished with a protective wood stain that gives them a darker hue. Near the house, an unused side return is now home to a large log store built by Theresa's husband Tom using cast-aside and collected wood scraps.

Next up is the exterior dining space. Bolster pads soften the bench seating, and the refectory table is decorated with candles and flowers. The scene would be just at home inside, save for the beautiful parasol.

Continuing up the garden, a bench provides a rest point not just for the eye. This is a moveable seating option should the family need the lawn space for play or pastimes. The bench has a timeless silhouette and its wooden surface can be updated and recoloured when necessary.

ABOVE
A practical refectory-style table features in the outside dining space. With a mixture of bench seating, it is a neat and robust solution that can easily handle unexpected extra diners. When dressed down, it offers a simple setting for relaxed family meals, morning coffee and low-key occasions, or for more formal events it can be effortlessly transformed with a tablecloth and cushions.

"A confident use of pattern and Theresa's signature tonal colour scheme clearly mark the way for this outdoor room to be used and appreciated."

The mid-section of the garden gives way to planters and fruit and vegetable beds. Growing at home is enjoyed by all ages and family favourites such as salad leaves and berries are tended by the children as much as the grown-ups. The raised height of the beds makes gardening more comfortable, with the side edges providing a place to perch. Coated in black paint, they bring a smart look to the hobby area and contrast with the lawn and hedge greenery.

The latter part of the garden is occupied by a shed and summer house. Styled as an inviting retreat at the end of the lawn, this probably once-ordinary garden building has been transformed by Theresa and her family. Its bright white painted exterior gleams in front of a backdrop of foliage. With enticing seating outside and in, it is the perfect escape pod in which to seek sanctuary. Inside, the furnishings offer a subtle nod to vintage style with an elegant collection of porcelain and pottery, as well as soft cotton fabrics featuring delicate floral designs. Various understated homely touches, such as prints and artwork, books and mirrors, suggest that this is a quieter space intended for peaceful unwinding.

It is in the summer house that many of the family's craft projects can be seen: a feature tiled floor, a stencilled rug, wall hangings, cut-flower posies and a handmade wreath. Many of these ideas have been undertaken by Theresa with the aid of her young children, demonstrating that there are opportunities to take part in the creative process at all ages. From refashioning furniture to applying detailing on homewares, it is a family affair that unites them all and adds a personal touch to the garden.

RIGHT

The summer house is a welcome haven at the end of Theresa's garden, providing opportunities for quiet contemplation away from the hustle and bustle near the back door. It is sited on a deck of scaffolding planks, where occasional chairs have been set up to soak up the sunshine in front of the entrance. On the floor is a hand-finished rug featuring decorative stencilling.

LEFT
Simple homewares are displayed and treasured alongside decorative items, bringing a humble quality to the summer house. Offering an insight into the household's hobbies, pastimes and workaday rituals, their modest features add character and individuality to the space. Here, Theresa has hung a charming broom on the panelled wall, where it complements her handmade wreath and felted wall hanging.

Despite the zoning, some common threads are interlaced throughout the whole garden. There are many festoon garlands and lanterns (electric versions near the house and solar-powered styles towards the end), and a cohesive colour scheme. Thanks to Theresa's flexible approach to styling, souvenirs and collections can be moved easily from house to garden and back again. The blurring of boundaries between inside and out means there is a perfect place for every guest to make themselves at home.

OPPOSITE
In order to make the best use of space, a daybed was custom made by hand to be a perfect fit for the summer house. Complete with padding and cushions, it is the ideal place for the children to relax or a spot to escape to for a secret snooze.

RIGHT
Mixing vintage looks with her bohemian styling, Theresa has decorated this room slowly over time so that it represents a continuous process of interiors exploration. Furniture is repainted when tired, humble homewares revamped and worn surfaces freshened up with handmade touches and detailing.

LEFT
Outdoor illumination
is provided by candles,
tealights and bistro lights.
Here, a group of hanging
lanterns and candlesticks
is just visible among the
foliage. One of the benefits
of having smaller, more
enclosed outdoor spaces
is that you can fill them
with lush greenery and
scented flowers.

POCKET *paradise*

A lover of cozy corners, Sarah Clark has created a pair of bijou courtyard gardens at the front and rear of her house. Serving as a life-enhancing antidote to the stresses of city living, these small but perfectly formed squares are all she needs for intimate gatherings and friendly get-togethers.

The front terrace is an open space, like a public piazza, while a more secluded secret plot can be found behind the house. Both are used for a variety of occasions, from morning meetings to down-tools drinks, and despite their size there is room for all. Scale-enhancing mirrors and lighting open up and brighten both areas. When visiting other people's gardens, Sarah often feels inspired by the wild, untamed features, so she has recreated some of these in her own space. For her it is all about mismatched details and a casual colour palette that changes with the seasons.

By introducing foliage, Sarah has used the walls as much as the floors to soften the hard landscaping. A once-bare wall in the rear courtyard is now covered with greenery and festoon lights. Trellises support the creepers on the parallel house wall and a staged planter space on the enclosed balcony above helps to draw the eye upwards.

LEFT
A bench has been installed
near the front door with
subtle, low-level lighting in
the adjacent beds. These
sensory elements are all the
more important in a small
space and can be enjoyed in
comfort thanks to cushions
brought out from indoors.

OPPOSITE
Soon after the family moved in,
Sarah went to town on plants
with which to fill up the bare
garden. The rear terrace is now
enveloped by vertical planting.
She made the trellis from wire
mesh, which is normally used
to reinforce concrete and is
sure to age beautifully.

LEFT
To create a welcoming and warming atmosphere all year round, a firepit has been installed in the larger courtyard at the front of the house. It is a magnet for visitors and family alike, who gather round to enjoy the warmth and light.

Now that she has a place to sit and enjoy the planting, Sarah is quite specific about the flowers and foliage she brings into the garden, particularly in the smaller rear courtyard. Plants are selected for personal reasons to evoke specific memories in a palette of muted green, white and blush. The colours have a calming and relaxing effect, and also connect the family to the seasons. They all find nature incredibly grounding, so the abundance of greenery is welcomed in for the mindful and biophilic benefits it bestows. Sarah has also tapped into the soothing potential of sound, with gentle tinkles and swishes from chimes and leafy boughs. Twinkling candlelight and the warm glow of flames in the firepit complete the scene.

The space is just as enticing for all manner of wildlife, with feeders to invite them in and a pond project underway. A suburban oasis for all, the garden is a gorgeous crowd pleaser on a small scale.

RIGHT
When Sarah and her family landscaped the front terrace, they relocated all the existing plants elsewhere in the garden. They also replaced a patch of muddy grass with paving stones taken from elsewhere. Rather than lose the amphibians that had made this area their home, they sourced a trough and spout from reclamation yards and installed a water feature for them in the low bed on the right, where it is partially obscured by foliage.

The main patio area is the perfect place for year-round relaxation. Surrounded by tall, well-established trees, it is very private, not overlooked and always peaceful with lots of visiting birds. It is Rasa's favourite spot to sit and reflect at the start of the day.

RIGHT & BELOW RIGHT

There are many collected pots dotted around the garden, suggesting strength in numbers. Here, a gathering of terracotta planters on a table brings together an assortment of plants with logs handily stored below. The table and a nearby stepladder divide the patio from the lawn.

VINTAGE *vibe*

Cozy and calming, Rasa T-Brasiene's garden is the place to be for old-school relaxation surrounded by stylishly salvaged materials. Leisurely lazing on the found, foraged and refurbished furniture is positively encouraged.

Finding contentment in rehoming and reconditioning, Rasa is a great believer in using second-hand finds in her home. Her appreciation of laidback living extends to the garden, where she has created spaces for her family to engage with and enjoy. They live outside as much as they can and love to host gatherings of loved ones.

Hidden from view by the surrounding greenery, the suburban plot feels exclusive yet welcoming. Unless invited in, you would never know it was there. Inside there are two patios, a lawn enclosed by trees, a greenhouse and the beginnings of a summer retreat. Industrious Rasa always has a project on the go.

The areas work cohesively together thanks to Rasa's use of rustic textures and muted colours. Natural materials prevail in the form of wood, wicker, dried grasses and leaves. Softer touches include hemps, woollen weaves and organic cottons. It is a very green garden peppered with white flowers, so the neutral furnishings balance the freshness perfectly.

Delicate petal shades and the hues of fading flowers are reflected in Rasa's tonal palette, which also mirrors the seasons. In the spring and summer, soft neutrals and blush pinks predominate, autumn introduces rustic browns while winter sees frosted whites and cooler tones. The colours tie the family back to nature, which can be enjoyed across the senses. Gentle music sometimes flows across the lawn to join in with the birdsong, but at other times Rasa appreciates how the sheltering trees can muffle everyday noise and create a tranquil space.

Much of the garden furniture has been upcycled and repurposed. Vintage sellers, salvage yards and second-hand sales are scoured for the discarded and redundant. There are hand-me-downs donated by friends and family and handmade projects created from old materials or redesigned to suit the setting. Turning her hand to all kinds of skills and crafts, Rasa repaints, reupholsters and repairs. She always finds the process fulfilling and takes pride in the transformation.

RIGHT
Blurring the boundary between indoor use and out, formerly housebound shelving has been cleaned and sealed before finding a new home outside. Eco-friendly outdoor varnishes, stains and paints are now available in a wide range of shades and finishes.

OPPOSITE & LEFT
The dining table was a DIY project and has been created from upcycled pallet wood and trestle legs donated by a neighbour. A rug has been installed underneath to cover inherited pavers. The table is laid with plates and platters sourced from vintage shops and second-hand fairs. There is a charm in the mismatched pieces that contributes to the relaxed styling.

LEFT
Proving that almost everything and anything can be collected and displayed, these neatly stacked logs look pleasingly humble on open shelves. The logs are sourced locally and add welcome weight to the lower part of the storage unit, making it more stable.

RIGHT
Rasa has cleverly used her collections and furniture to hide and disguise the exterior walls of the house. Her old dining table has been sawn in half to create vertical staging for pots, earthenware vessels, plants and decorative accessories. Painted a similar grey shade to the wall, the structure blends into the background, allowing the arrangement of objects to take the spotlight. The house-shaped candle holders look beautiful in the evening.

"Turning her hand to all kinds of skills and crafts, Rasa repaints, reupholsters and repairs. She finds the process fulfilling and takes pride in the transformation."

Equally important is the act of cherishing and appreciating the existing elements: pausing before digging up or ripping back, reflecting how something could be altered or covered up if not quite right. It is a matter of valuing inherited structures and surfaces and recognizing their worth. Rasa takes a sustainable approach not only when introducing items to her home and garden but also in her treatment of that which was already there. In particular, she has avoided expensive and potentially unnecessary upheaval such as hard landscaping unless she can reuse the waste materials elsewhere.

Rasa often brings pieces from the house outside and, as long as they are treated to cope with the elements, they are a happy fit in the garden. The space has an easy flow of considered characteristics. Thanks to the wholesome, hearty ambience that Rasa has brought forth, quality times are to be had in this remarkable setting.

OPEN *house*

Lending character to a garden still relatively in its infancy can be difficult, but Isatu Chadborn and her family have really embraced the challenge. Inheriting a somewhat blank canvas at their back door gave them the opportunity to fashion and shape the space to their own requirements.

From the outset, Isatu had a clear idea of how she wanted to spend her time outside. This saved effort during the planning phase, allowing her to focus on creating a sociable space with a variety of entertaining options. The garden naturally became an extension of her happy home – and, amazingly, most of the proposed changes took place in under two years.

Thanks to Isatu's timeless sense of style, the different spaces relate to one another yet each has its own atmosphere. The overall aesthetic is an elegant blend of Scandinavian, Japanese and mid-century elements. These form a laidback and easy-going backdrop for convivial outdoor gatherings. The colour scheme also promotes a warm and inviting ambience.

RIGHT
A central cookout space presides over the garden. Created from a collection of new and old materials, it shelters an upcycled work bench and the family's existing dining chairs. The basin is plumbed into a system of drainpipes so that Isatu can wash dishes and pot up plants using collected rainwater.

OPPOSITE
Sleek modular seating suits the garden's modern aesthetic and is ideal when welcoming unexpected visitors. Purpose-made outdoor furniture in durable pressure-treated wood or painted metal gives year-round satisfaction. Isatu has installed a retractable awning to extend the lifespan of less robust indoor-outdoor pieces.

New developments in all-weather fabric upholstery and textiles keep soft furnishings looking at their best.

ABOVE
Isatu took a creative, contemporary approach to the garden design, which demonstrates a number of refreshing and innovative yet easily achievable ideas within the comfortable open-plan setting.

The garden is divided into zones, which include areas for lounging and dining as well as a summer house. A potting shed towards the front of the property is a more recent addition. They are all favourite spaces for Isatu to spend time in. Activities such as cooking in the outdoor kitchen, enjoying the company of friends at the dining table, cozying up near the fireside or leisurely winding down in the summer house or potting shed are all an extension of how she lives and whiles away the time in her home.

LEFT

Inspired by her love of cooking and entertaining and with a typically can-do attitude, Isatu has created a very personal and inviting outdoor kitchen, which she now loves to share with guests. A reclaimed basin and work bench have been upcycled and are practical additions to the space.

RIGHT

Indoor and outdoor spaces are cleverly connected by the same monochromatic colour palette and simple textures. Whitewashed panels, smooth pavers, wicker and varying tones of wood easily shift between the two areas for an effect that is uniform but still relaxed. Greenery in portable pots brings lush textures.

A keen upcycler, Isatu has brought many reclaimed resources into the main garden as well as giving its existing features a new lease of life. She and her husband Pete flipped over the original curved decking, changed the shape to a rectangle and painted it black. They trimmed down and repainted the remaining fence panels, too. A vintage butler's sink was purchased from a local reclamation yard for the outdoor kitchen, and Pete installed drainpipes and guttering in order to have running rainwater for dish washing and potting plants. The kitchen counter started its life as a work bench and has been painted and smartened up.

LEFT

There are many indoor homewares used outside to link the house and garden, soften the hard landscaping and bring an 'outdoor room' feel to the space.

"Moving furniture indoors and out as needed proved to be a wonderful way to repurpose or restyle familiar pieces."

Isatu and Pete shopped and trawled their home for items with which to furnish the summer house and dining area. Moving furniture indoors and out as needed proved to be a wonderful way to repurpose or restyle familiar pieces that they already owned. Mixing old with new in this way always helps to make a home feel unique, too.

Thrift shops, vintage emporiums, reclamation yards and online marketplaces were all invaluable sources of interesting pieces in search of a new home. Each has a wonderful history behind it and making use of these unloved or unwanted items feels much more meaningful and personal than purchasing brand new.

PAGE 112

Isatu has made the most of every potential seating nook in and around the garden. This forgotten corner has become an enviable place to rest and observe the garden from a shaded swing chair.

PAGE 113

Rather than throw away the existing decking, Isatu and Pete turned over and repainted the panels using an eco-friendly wood stain. Gravel borders link the exterior spaces together.

Further building and finishing materials came from yards or even delivery packaging. Scaffolding boards have been reused and pallet wood repurposed. The potting shed incorporates windows and doors taken out of the house during previous renovation projects. Although neither vintage nor distinct in design, these reclaimed materials still have years of use left in them.

Isatu shares a bond with plants, appreciating the character they lend to a home as well as their effect on her wellbeing. She favours simple planting in order to enjoy each and every specimen. In the border area, her beloved stems and shoots now take pride of place, with a line of silver birch trees for screening and shade. There are plenty of pots to move around, too, filling gaps with greenery or enriching the air with sound, silhouette and scent. Flowers to attract pollinators, trees and a nesting box to entice birds all encourage biodiversity. Supporting the environment in a suburban garden is an uplifting experience.

The garden has become a place for the family to enjoy spending time together, in spring, summer and beyond. By resourcefully repurposing materials and introducing fluidity between the different areas, Isatu has created a simple, soulful legacy that will age perfectly with time.

OPPOSITE

A recent addition to the garden, the potting shed was constructed by Isatu and Pete using old windowpanes reclaimed from other house projects – the wall has simply been built around them.

ABOVE

With a mostly glazed wall and clear rooflight ceiling, there is plenty of light coming into the new space. Its internal framework creates neat open shelves on the wall. A reclaimed sink has been fitted for potting up.

RIGHT

Further shelving has been made from wooden offcuts, with a row of pegs for garden tools. The mismatched shelves are the perfect place for flowerpots and gardenalia, including former food dishes that have been repurposed as pot saucers.

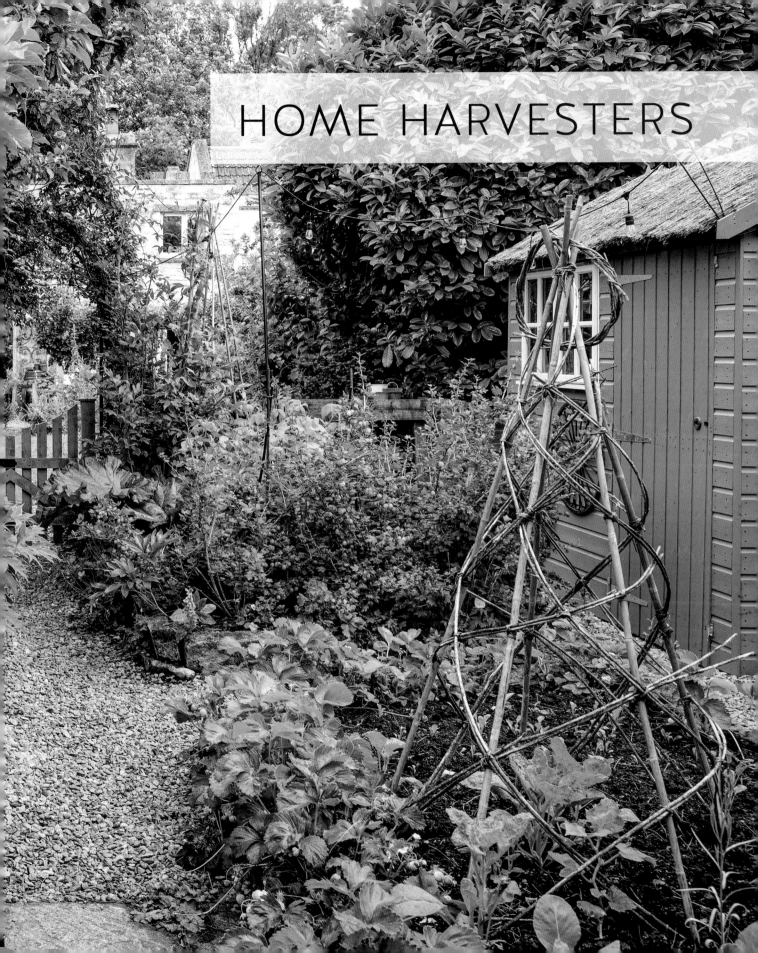

MAGICAL
gathering

Having evolved from its cottage-garden origins, Nyla Abraham's collection of pretty corner patches blends her personal ideals into a truly enchanting suburban backyard.

Nyla's aim was to recreate the gardens of her childhood imagination. The clever planting and styling ideas tell of her love of home-grown produce, upcycling and the romance of what might be around the next corner. It is a place of discovery and adventure for her family to enjoy.

ABOVE & OPPOSITE
There is a gravel garden at the front of the plot with a feeding table to attract birds. This is placed near a window and offers the chance to watch the wildlife from indoors. Hostas and ferns in pots are moved around the garden as needed.

LEFT
A miniature greenhouse has been raised up to a more comfortable height. The crates were sourced and decorated for Nyla's wedding to her husband Paul. They are now used for garden projects.

OPPOSITE

Nyla uses vintage pots and other containers to grow vegetables in the allotment, with supports made using coppiced wood from a relative's garden. Having enjoyed discovering how to cultivate home-grown produce, she cares a lot about doing so sustainably and ethically. She recently decided to propagate most of her own plants, all of which are grown organically.

LEFT & BELOW

For some things, practicality reigns over prettiness. One such area is the potting bench, which embodies Nyla's wholesome values. It comprises an upcycled kitchen sink and drainer supported by a framework of recycled wooden pallets and railway sleepers/railroad ties. The nearby compost bin is concealed between the shed and a leafy laurel tree.

The garden forms an L shape around Nyla's cottage with a formal arrangement of espalier trees and trellises at the front to greet guests as they arrive. Through an arch, the main garden begins with a fine fern shrubbery established around a wall. Allowing the greenery to flow onto and blend in with the gravel has blurred the hard landscaping for a softer look.

Here, we are first introduced to Nyla and her husband Paul's creative thinking. There is a handmade woodshed on the side, and around the corner a vintage miniature greenhouse and a collection of upcycled crates. Water butts are placed to collect rainwater and there is a bird table to attract wildlife. Reclaimed kitchen chairs and a table made from wooden pallets offer an immediate place to perch outside the house. Assorted pots are planted with herbs and succulents, and there are built-in cupboards to house garden essentials. The handmade fencing was crafted by Paul using foraged wood. Beautiful borders adorn the lawn, but it s beyond the next archway that the real jewel of the garden can be found: the allotment.

RIGHT

Homewares such as this clock are dotted around the garden rather than left forgotten inside the house.

FAR RIGHT

Nyla has installed several bug houses to attract a variety of insects. A log or pile of leaves can serve as an alternative to a purpose-built house like this one.

BELOW

On the patio, a vintage chiminea has a timeworn look after years of weathering. Nyla has let greenery creep into the pavement cracks for an organic feel.

This productive plot is the main hub of the garden, with various work stations and potting areas around the raised beds. Planting at various levels allows Nyla's young daughter to help care for the ground-loving herbs and salad leaves, as well as the climbing legumes on their willow wigwams. Deep-rooted vegetables thrive in old metal bathtubs and water tanks.

A renovated folly is used for growing on, with a new large window to let in plenty of light. A shed to the side has had its felt roof covered with a roll of thatch screening. It houses a practical potting bench made from upcycled pallets and an old sink.

OPPOSITE

Many of the garden's structures are the handiwork of Paul, who built this garden shelter out of reclaimed wood and the shingles from an old fence panel. Painted with an eco-friendly stain, it will last for years. The wicker bench has been made snug with an old blanket and cushions.

At the back of the allotment is a tiny sheltered terrace, just large enough to accommodate a vintage wicker sofa. An old chiminea is kept here for use on chillier days or evenings and feathery wisteria nods pleasantly in the breeze. Paul's dedicated tool shed can also be found here and is entered by another charming door.

The terrace looks out onto the allotment and also a dedicated outdoor dining space. Hedging and grass here are left long so that the greenery can add softness, while fruit trees bring leafy cover to the area not covered by the parasol over the dining table. This rear section of the plot is a private space, a secret only shared by Nyla's family.

Nature is everything to Nyla and being outdoors allows her to connect with her surroundings. She especially enjoys the roofless experience of seeing the ground reach up to the sky. The garden is as free-spirited as its owners, and is allowed to grow as nature intended while producing food for the family. It represents a marriage of gardening leisure and pleasure, an opportunity to share made-in-heaven moments and priceless experiences.

ABOVE

The dining table and chairs were bought second hand and have been refreshed with a new paint colour. Metal furniture is ideal for a project of this kind. Remove any rust with a wire brush and wipe down the surface, then add a couple of coats of eco-friendly metal paint. Using a brush is an easier method, or you can use non-toxic spray paint for a smoother finish.

LEFT

A charming upcycling idea is to reinvent old china. Rub the surfaces with sandpaper for grip before glueing them together. Drill a few holes, thread a chain through and hang up your new planter.

BELOW LEFT

Sculptural stakes topped with metal discs have been interspersed along the flower borders. They introduce regularity as well as textural and visual interest. The discs also gather water on rainy days, allowing wildlife to stop and sip.

BELOW

A coffee table has been made from an upcycled wooden pallet with hairpin legs attached to the underside. This is a brilliant way to reinvent old packaging instead of discarding it. Knocks and dents are part of its appeal.

"The garden is as free-spirited as its owners, and is allowed to grow as nature intended while producing food for the family."

PLOT *to plate*

Craftsman and cultivator Rob Cowan has created a potager patch from farmyard enclosures and backdoor boundaries. A confident builder and maker, he has recycled discarded objects into growing spaces and cookout corners in which to enjoy the fresh and abundant harvest.

Rob rents his cottage and garden from a local farmer and has taken full advantage of their rural location. The main flower garden is to the side of the cottage, and he has also installed raised beds and planters on patches of waste ground around the farm outbuildings and along the entry lane. Not only productive, these growing spaces are a great distraction from life's stresses, and there is never a short supply of Rob's favourite fruit and veg.

Working on the rambling garden immediately to the side of their home has been a real labour of love for him and his family. First of all, there is a patio seating area furnished with a bench and dining table. A gate in the fence to the side leads to a pretty flower garden. This doubles as an outdoor eatery with a wood-fired oven, which Rob built himself, and space for food preparation.

OPPOSITE

A simple but sturdy tool shed stands guard over the rear allotment patch. Mismatched furniture from the house now serves as a potting bench and seating. The farm building to the side has been used as informal storage space for tools and tackle, and provides shelter during inclement weather.

RIGHT

An old tea chest has been potted up with tomatoes. At one point there was a tomato border next to the wood-fired stove, so the transition from picking to grilling could be done in seconds.

RIGHT

All the fencing has been made by Rob using coppiced wood, including this charming gate. The naturally formed knots and imperfections lend a lovely character to the finished fencing. Not just there for prettiness, the boundary keeps the chickens off the lawn and protects the floral borders.

Out beyond more fencing is the working garden, where a wealth of growing ideas keeps the food cycle in motion. The site has been divided into allotment, propagation spaces, tool sheds and potting benches. There is a chicken coop and a place to store the materials and found items that Rob uses for upcycling projects.

The family are passionate fixer-uppers and love the vibe of vintage pieces. Not just content with simple homemade projects, they often rethink or refashion reclaimed items into something useful and considered.

ABOVE LEFT
Kitchenalia can make for great planters, especially when a piece has its own built-in drainage holes as seen in this colander. Look out at second-hand or vintage fairs for outsized catering versions, which can accommodate more prolific planting.

LEFT
Rob's outdoor kitchen space has been cleverly made from wooden offcuts and unwanted furniture. Panelling, posts, ladders and bookends have all been fitted together to create this external prep and storage space.

ABOVE RIGHT
The bespoke wood-fired brick oven was made by Rob and has been a great success. Rob now has a small business crafting similar ovens for the general public. Lucky neighbours, drawn by the most amazing cooking aromas, are regularly treated to personalized pizzas. Rob has also experimented with various other dishes and is constantly widening his recipe repertoire.

Old wooden pallets, poles, boards, furniture elements and everything in between now pops up in Rob's garden as a shelving structure, fencing feature, plant trough or wall tidy. He has even turned his hand to garden accessories, such as lighting and candle sconces. Every corner offers something to catch the eye.

Not to be forgotten, the wildlife is also well looked after thanks to a variety of handcrafted sanctuaries. Cubbies, dens and boltholes for mini beasts and bird are positioned around the plot. Most have been constructed from oddments and leftover materials, but each has been crafted with love and finished to perfection.

The whole garden is regularly used and enjoyed by Rob's family, friends and neighbours, the biggest draw being the outdoor wood-fired stove, which was made bespoke by Rob himself. Each brick in the central dome was carefully selected and placed by hand to create the curved structure. The main oven is housed behind wooden cladding with a stove pipe protruding from the front. To finish, Rob made an oven door by welding together part of a metal cabinet with a baking tray. It works a treat and is very popular with the neighbours who stop by for pizzas and more.

The garden is a beautiful blend of pretty and practical, and is a testament to the family for what can be achieved in a rented space over just a few years. Offering an abundance of gorgeous flowers and mouth-watering home-grown delicacies, it really is a garden to feed the soul.

ABOVE
The chickens are in their element in Rob's garden with the amount of vegetables he grows. They keep the slugs and snails at bay, so they are free to roam despite occasionally nibbling the crops.

ABOVE
A planter made from an old fruit pallet houses beautiful flowers that cascade down the wall. A coat of white paint freshens and protects the wooden frame.

OPPOSITE
The garden is bordered by a stone wall, which absorbs the sun's rays and warms the plants in the adjacent border at the day's end. The tomato plants that once grew in this sunny spot have made way for flowering species.

LEFT
A set of wonderfully weathered vintage folding chairs surrounds the dining table on the patio. They have a charmingly timeworn appearance, and with the addition of a soft cushion or throw, they are the perfect place to sit and relax.

RICH *pickings*

Bringing joy and a fruitful return, Julia Parker's allotment and greenhouse reward her with far more than just their flowers and produce. Tending the plot offers mindful benefits, too, and her workshops help others to engage with the seasons and learn about gardening in a vibrant, colourful setting.

Central to the ethos behind the plot is how Julia gardens and the manner in which she cultivates and raises plants as well as what she grows. Although the allotment is divided into different sections – including crop-filled borders, the greenhouse, an orchard and fruit canes – each of these supplements the others in a supportive ecosystem. Julia designed the space as an outdoor classroom, which provides an active backdrop for her gardening workshops.

"There are only a couple of quieter months in this garden and Julia is kept busy planning, planting, potting and picking almost year round."

LEFT
Rather than needlessly buying new supports for plants, Julia prefers to make her own using repurposed materials and household objects. Coppiced branches, old canes, sticks and staves can easily be put together to create a sturdy framework for climbers. Save lengths of ribbon, shoelaces, wool and any kind of thread, as you can use these to tie everything together. Wear and tear will soften the form of these structures so that they age charmingly over time.

Borders and boundaries keep plots and beds orderly and provide shelter for fragile foliage and flowers. Low height levels also allow for views across the garden rather than totally screening off each area. The size also means they are easier to maintain than lofty hedges and leave the plots exposed to the sun and rain. Attracting wildlife to make themselves at home inside, they provide an accessible but dry space for butterflies and mini beasts to take refuge in adverse weather conditions or cocoon and isolate over winter.

Fondly called 'the veggie patch', the plot is tucked away from the main house and garden, and walking to it is always a welcome surprise. The current boundary wall is Victorian with an inherited lean-to greenhouse up against it. The building is blessed with, as Julia puts it, more than adequate ventilation, but the odd gap doesn't seem to bother the plants inside. The original aluminium frame has been repainted in a brightening shade of cream and, despite vintage heating pipes not quite functioning as they should, there is enough natural warmth and light to bring most things to fruition. In use throughout the year, the greenhouse extends the growing season so that the vegetable beds are kept brimming with bounty for as long as possible. There are only a couple of quieter months in this garden and Julia is kept busy planning, planting, potting and picking almost year round.

Creating the vegetable patch was rather like painting a picture. Having left city life behind, she missed the colour, contrast and spirit of her former home. The garden was a brilliant blank canvas on which to start afresh. Painting with plants, she has added bright hues, shapely silhouettes and natural contours using an attractive blend of fruit, vegetables and flowers. Annuals and perennials mark the seasons from first shoots to last seed heads. Things are left in the ground as needed or past flowering if they are able to give back to the garden and help the local wildlife.

OPPOSITE

A plant-growing powerhouse, the inherited greenhouse has raised generation after generation of new life and is the hub of the allotment's activities despite its age. The glazing may need a little TLC, but a coat of paint has freshened up the metal frame.

ABOVE

An assortment of coloured twine from sustainable brand Nutscene creates a humble yet homely display on open shelving in the greenhouse. The neat bundles are within easy and orderly reach and the different shades can be seen and enjoyed.

ABOVE RIGHT

The greenhouse was built against this handsome Victorian red-brick wall, which supports the glass and aluminium structure and helps to keep the plants warm. It is also the perfect place to hang up Julia's vintage gardenalia.

RIGHT

With a large amount of garden bits and pieces and ephemera to keep organised, Julia uses pots, cans and jars as versatile storage. They hold seeds, plant markers and propagation tools, and can be used as planters for seedlings, too.

RIGHT

Tin can planters are perfect for herbs and greens. A mix of cans of different volumes, including larger catering-sized versions, gives a broader scope to the plants that can be grown. The exterior labels lend colour and interest to the arrangement.

FAR RIGHT

Giving a new spin on an old idea comes easily to Julia. These plant markers are made from pruned branches, which she has trimmed and painted to create a flat surface on which to label plant varieties.

Julia believes gardening should be for all, and she is always looking for cost-effective, resourceful and eco-friendly ways to get the most out of her garden, from sharing seeds to taking cuttings and upcycling containers. She often plants single crops and lets them go to seed, allowing her to germinate more plants for the following season. She recalls letting a single root vegetable go over for the sake of gathering the ensuing flower heads and explains that she finds all these experiences incredibly satisfying.

There is also the chance to share spent harvests with the birds and mini beasts. Julia invites the pollinators into her patch by planting their favourite flowers to increase productivity and support the environment.

LEFT & OPPOSITE

The greenhouse is a place where Julia can unwind and be herself surrounded by all her favourite things. It is filled with personal touches that reflect Julia's likes, interests and habits. Although neatly stowed on the wall shelves and work bench, these are easily accessible while she works. Plants mingle freely among the miscellaneous collections and upcycled objects, adding to the joyfully eclectic atmosphere.

OPPOSITE & ABOVE
Lit by a rustic chandelier, a tree bench in the orchard provides a pretty place to rest and admire the garden. This neat seating arrangement is perfect for smaller gardens or areas where space is tight. Choose a bench that is easy to maintain and will still be large enough to accommodate the tree when it has reached its full size.

ABOVE RIGHT
Wooden trugs have long been the basket of choice for many gardeners. They are perfect for caddying plants and tools, and they age beautifully.

Most of the containers started life as something else around the home, whether as now-redundant packaging or as other humdrum bits and pieces. Paper towel rolls, tubs, bags and cans are upcycled and find a new home in the garden. It is a brilliant way to reduce waste and can lead to creative or amusing possibilities. Old shoes can be reused as planters for herbs, saucepans are the perfect receptacles to grow on cuttings and there are millions of ways to plant up jam jars and old crocks.

Tapped to make the most of its local resources, the landscape has been thoroughly explored with this garden. Water butts collect rainfall and by working with the weather, mulching the ground, creating dew pockets and establishing plant cover, Julia has ensured that the soil remains moist for longer. The vegetables only need watering in a drought and the only plants that receive pure tap water are the seedlings in the greenhouse. The plants are the better for it; growing deeper roots and working harder to survive has made them more robust.

The grounds certainly give back to Julia in abundance and it is a mutually beneficial relationship. Her ethos is all about nurturing in harmony with nature and growing with sustainability in mind. In this thriving and productive garden, cultivating is a shared experience with biophilic and back-to-nature benefits.

DAY DREAMERS

LEFT & OPPOSITE
The reclaimed deck occupies what used to be a concrete paved area with a wall that blocked light into the living room. Kay's family knocked down the wall and local builders laid the wood and built a corner seat from reclaimed boards. The flower beds were designed by Kay.

BELOW LEFT
Inspired by memories of playing games together during family holidays, Kay built a pétanque pit alongside the house as a present to her husband Andy for their tin wedding anniversary. It was perhaps a tenuous link, but much appreciated by him.

PERFECTLY *imperfect*

Created as an extension of her home, Kay Prestney's garden is a natural and relaxed environment in which to lose oneself and while away the hours.

Kay's imaginative and artistic design has plenty of thoughtful and soulful corners to discover and sustainable schemes to unearth. Featuring ideas inspired by family holidays and outings, the garden offers a chance to disconnect and wind down.

This calming garden is a place to visit to be able to let go instantly, lighten up and recharge. It provides moments to enjoy the seasons, observe the latest flower to bloom, listen to birdsong or share food, laughter and good times as a family.

Kay also feels a sense of pride looking at the projects she has undertaken in the garden. After the adventures of upcycling and making good unwelcome or unloved features, she can now enjoy the results.

The garden is an inspiring example of a sustainably created setting, featuring pallet and scaffolding boards and railway sleepers/railroad ties repurposed as edging and furniture. There are zones for living, dining and gaming, plus a greenhouse and a garden room. Kay's ingenuity is most apparent in the garden room, which she designed and created with a skilled maker using found materials and architectural salvage. The challenging build was educational, teaching Kay practical skills as well as patience, self-discovery and the importance of enjoying the process.

ABOVE LEFT
A drinks table has been constructed from an old trolley base topped with a slab of reclaimed marble. The pétanque scoreboard was made from a picture frame and a piece of MDF painted with chalkboard paint.

ABOVE
These lights run on solar power. You could make a simpler version using regular cans painted in your chosen colours – stamp out holes with a nail and pop a candle inside.

LEFT
There are abundant fruit trees and canes around the garden, including this fig tree. Herbs feature prominently, too. The couple both love to cook and often send the children outside to identify and pick herbs for dinner.

There are lots of sentimental additions and hand-me-down heirlooms in the garden room, including an old strawberry grading table that was used on Andy's childhood farm. The daybed was a kind gift from a friend whose daughter had outgrown it. Dressed in vintage linens, it is Kay's favourite place to snooze.

PAGE 145

Instead of buying a new garden room, Kay chose to build her own using second-hand materials. There is a story behind every single piece. The back wall was made from a set of three reclaimed doors, which were bought via an online marketplace from a couple who had used them as a backdrop for their wedding photos. The huge Georgian sash windows came from an architectural salvage warehouse.

RIGHT & BELOW RIGHT

Textures are aplenty in the room, for example in the dried flowers and foliage hanging from the ceiling or placed in vases. Foraged from the garden or the family's rewilding field, they evoke memories of when and where they were found.

ABOVE

The garden room connects to the outside space with the copious amount of glazing in its assortment of doors and windows. Kay was not worried about totally sealing it off from the elements, so the salvaged materials fit together with a few gaps in order to keep them in their original state.

Kay has taken every opportunity to make the garden as eco-friendly as possible. The lanterns are solar powered, and while the festoons run off the mains grid, they are powered by a green energy provider so that all the electricity is generated by wind or water turbines. Rainwater is collected in water butts and galvanized bathtubs around the garden, in which vintage watering cans can be dipped. When not in use, these are left around the garden for display.

The garden's evolution has changed the way the family use the space and make memories throughout the year. Above all, they spend much more time outside nowadays. The deck is an inviting place for relaxation, blending seamlessly with the wooden floor in the living room. The garden room is a workspace away from the constraints of indoor living. And the garden as a whole is a place of meaning, with plants and features added in celebration of beloved people and places.

COUNTRY *idyll*

Samantha Greetham lives the garden dream with her family, dogs and chickens in a utopian, away-from-it-all plot. Filled with life-enriching collections, it is a place that distracts from everyday worries and eases the mind.

Thanks to a combination of clever design and patience, Samantha has created a truly joyful garden. What was originally purchased for its solitary and still location has been reimagined to become a sensual place in which to lose oneself. After spending many years investing in her thatched cottage, she turned her hand to the garden beyond to create a sympathetic partner space.

ABOVE

The greenhouse is Samantha's favourite space in the garden and is where she can usually be found. It is a place for pottering and planting, discovering and doing. Plants are tended for inside and out. It is a hub of activity.

OPPOSITE

Built from oak, the greenhouse has been painted in a creamy white and looks fresh against the greenery. Hazel hurdles fence off this area, with access via a gate. Samantha used locally sourced branches to make the wreath, a homespun detail that will age beautifully over the years.

The garden has been divided into smaller courtyards and corners. Hazel hurdles, picket fencing, hedging and shrubs all have been used to create quiet quarters, with a bank at the rear of the house supplying interest on different levels. Each area has been further partitioned with raised beds, borders and trellises, and there are trails and tracks throughout. This technique tricks the eye into thinking that the plot is much larger than it really is while carving the garden into distinct areas and sectioning off what each part of the grounds could be used for.

One of these zones is the working garden, which houses Samantha's greenhouse – a hive of activity, it is her favourite place in the garden and definitely the hub where she spends most of her time. Made of oak by her talented local builder, the structure has a homely quality and features many potting-up and growing-on collections and wares. Seeds are sown, tender plants are lovingly looked after and the gardening year is planned to perfection. When the weather turns, it serves as a handy covered space and is often visited by Samantha's chickens, a charming variety of breeds. There is always company to be found in the garden, whether from family, friends, pets or visiting wildlife. Right outside the greenhouse, raised beds and fruit trees bring pollinators and productive winged insects into the back garden.

OPPOSITE & ABOVE RIGHT

The outdoor dining area is the place to be for sundowners. The reclaimed decking looks resplendent in the ebbing sunlight, with shadows and dapples playing across its surface. It is teamed with many other salvaged and recycled fittings in this area, all of which lend a homely look to the space.

RIGHT

A trolley is the perfect portable furniture piece for transporting homewares and accessories from house to garden and back again. Samantha also uses hers for plants and general storage, and it often serves as a place where she can display and arrange cut flowers and herbs.

LEFT & OPPOSITE

This area near the dining table is a decadent space to pre-dinner drinks or casual cocktails. Equally well suited for sunbathing and stargazing, a pair of armchairs offer comfy seating with the aid of plump cushions, which are brought in and out of the house as needed. When not in use, the firepit is stocked with candles for evening illumination.

BELOW

A deep-seated bench with cushions is always an inviting place to sit, and the size of this one makes it ideal for creating and making, too. The canopy of the cherry tree keeps this area cool and a charming rope swing is suspended from one of the branches.

Echoing the make-up and materials of the cottage, a divine and unique thatched summer house was added during the transformation of the garden. In front of this, a sensational scented lavender and rose garden prevails. Samantha's favourite varieties for picking include the rose 'Tranquillity' and the pompom-shaped flower heads of *Hydrangea arborescens* 'Annabelle'. The flowers nod elegantly to each other in the breeze, as if chatting in agreement of ongoing concerns. Samantha has many plans for this area, including gates, rose arches and even a water feature. For now, though, the sight and scent of the blooms is a great pleasure.

Immediately off from the rear of the cottage is the garden room, made from locally sourced oak, reclaimed scaffold boards and beautiful old pantiles from a barn in a nearby village. Wisteria scrambles over the rooftop and jasmine climbs up the lean-to structure, which nestles down in an earth bank. From the kitchen entrance, the cottage looks as though it is slowly being swallowed up by the garden.

*"There is always
company to be
found in the
garden, whether
from family,
friends, pets or
visiting wildlife."*

LEFT

A lean-to garden room leads off from the kitchen. Made from reclaimed oak, scaffolding boards and pantiles, it is a snug, sheltered space with an indoor-outdoor vibe. Homewares are protected, table linens sheltered and furniture cosseted by the well-worn structure.

OPPOSITE ABOVE LEFT

Recycled wooden panelling makes a wonderful backdrop for rough-hewn logs and a handmade wreath.

OPPOSITE ABOVE RIGHT

Mismatched chairs are used for casual dining in the garden room. Watering cans, candles and plants are arranged on rustic shelves and an upcycled bench.

OPPOSITE BELOW LEFT

Railway sleepers/railroad ties hold back earthworks around the sunken garden room. The floor is made of scaffolding boards. Lush planting makes the space feel connected to its surroundings, as though the garden is creeping in to provide shelter from the elements.

OPPOSITE BELOW RIGHT

The chipped paintwork of a vintage dresser/hutch looks better with age. Samantha keeps modest indoor seating out here all year round. This armchair has slip covers that are easy to clean, and she likes to vary the throws and cushions.

A decked area leads to the exterior dining and living space. Edged with reclaimed scaffolding boards, this part of the garden is raised to make the best of the views. Samantha is passionate about using locally sourced and recycled materials; all the bricks used to create paths around the plot were rescued from nearby. It is this space that has the most outstanding countryside views and enjoys the last of the warmth and light from the sun. The sunsets are spectacular and it is the perfect place to end the day with a smile.

Heavily scented, evocative and enchanting, Samantha's garden has a unique character and is filled with memories. One can easily find a quiet spot to sit and be. This place offers solace and gently restores with its charm and soul.

COTTAGE *core*

For Sharon Foskett, it is the pretty flowers she remembers from her childhood that have inspired her charming plot. Having always loved the look of cottage-garden planting, in which the borders seem to have been there forever, she has devoted herself to creating a rambling, romantic setting that appears to have sown and grown itself.

OPPOSITE
The rear gravel garden that opens up from the kitchen is the perfect spot for informal alfresco eating. A metal dining table and chairs set the scene for this area, which Sharon has dressed with a fringed parasol and paper bunting.

ABOVE & RIGHT
The summer house interior has been dressed in calming and cooling colours to create a balanced backdrop for all kinds of activities. Sometimes a work station, at other times a relaxing hideaway, it is a favourite space for all. The whitewashed boards are a wonderful backdrop for vintage finds.

Sharon inherited a completely blank canvas when she bought the plot: a muddy patch of ground wrapped around a humble and neglected fisherman's house. Being a gardening newcomer, she went with what she liked and pored over books and magazines for inspiration. A tight learning curve followed and, with much perseverance, what started as a levelling project involving a digger has produced her very own flower-filled paradise.

The garden is divided into sections, with openings and places to pause dotted throughout. An arbour in full bloom, a fragrant and fabulous taster of what is to come, welcomes visitors along the path to the front door. Along the side is a chicken run for Sharon's beloved hens, which supply her honesty-box egg house. A gate and lawn lead to children's play spaces and a potting bench beyond. There is room for a couple of dining tables, one positioned next to a

LEFT

The stove, made from an old keg, a pipe and parts of a helicopter engine, is a great example of creative upcycling. Made and welded together by Sharon's husband Cobie, it provides a place to share a drink and toast marshmallows when the night draws in.

LEFT

Sharon's daughter Pixie built this tepee using reclaimed wood. Pixie measured, cut, assembled and painted the timber as one of her first projects. It is now a fun shelter used by all the family. Cushions and throws are laid on the floor for comfort. It is a charming hideaway.

RIGHT

Sharon has divided up the rear of the garden by using different ground surfaces, including gravel in this dining space. Gravel is a practical choice for eating areas, especially as this is also where the stove is kept; a grassy surface underfoot could easily have become scorched. A fence and planter also help to break up the space. Pots and troughs can be planted with flowers and foliage of varying heights to create a natural partition.

homemade stove, then on to a summer house and shaded terrace at the rear. Each of these areas is surrounded by cut-and-come-again flowers, which Sharon often brings inside so that their abundance can be enjoyed at all times.

The wildlife is positively welcomed and encouraged to visit and stay. Plants are brought in with creatures in mind, especially pollinators. A rescued hedgehog once took up residence in the summer house to nurture her newborn hoglets, and the bug boxes scattered around the fences were bespoke made by Sharon's carpenter son. Birds are fed and those who stay have bijou boxes made by Sharon's husband using recycled wood.

A vintage table and chairs, sourced from various brocantes and fairs, are placed immediately outside the house. Sharon is a passionate upcycler and loves to restore and protect furniture for outdoor use. Using leftover varnishes, fabric oddments, a lick of paint here and some reupholstery there, she is able to bring a new look and individuality to these second-hand items.

FAR LEFT

One of Sharon's favourite finds, this old ceramic sink is living out a new life as a potting bench with a display of plants around its rim.

LEFT

An honesty-box egg house made from reclaimed wooden pallets greets visitors on the garden path that runs alongside the property.

BELOW

The dovecot was sourced from a second-hand fair before being cleaned up and installed. Sharon made the colourful flag using a patchwork of favourite vintage fabric remnants that she sewed together.

Sustainability is very important to Sharon, who sees great potential in the unwanted items she rescues from second-hand fairs and skips. She loves to reinvent these items into something new. Another eco-friendly touch is the mix of solar-powered lighting and candles that provides illumination for the evenings.

The summer house was one of the first additions to the garden. Nowadays it is enjoyed by all the family, whether for lively recreation or quiet downtime. It is also a place to which Sharon can withdraw to relax with sewing projects, a good book, music or just the calm of being alone. She enjoys listening to the weather or watching the world go by.

The natural light in and around the garden is glorious. It offers warming sun in the winter and shade during hot spells. Covered with a canopy of trees, the space is a secluded sanctuary for all. It has opened up a world of discovery for Sharon's children, with whom she can enjoy making precious memories of their early years.

Candles and watering cans are gathered together in a display that combines prettiness and practicality. Alison has invested in larger hurricanes and torches as well as tealights and votives for variety. The watering cans are in regular use from first sun to the last rays, so it is essential to keep them in an accessible place.

RIGHT

A snug sofa on the top terrace is arranged to make the best of the views, while leaving the French windows from the house clear to enjoy the vista, too. The area is dressed with comfortable cushions and throws, with decorative bunting for added colour.

NATURAL *secret*

A perfect slice of tropical paradise positioned in the middle of a city, Alison Bosworth's gorgeous garden offers her a fabulous getaway right on her doorstep. Established over many years, it still has many fresh and wonderful surprises to offer.

Having been allowed to evolve in a free and relaxed way, Alison's garden has a delightful sense of spontaneity. She drew inspiration from her deep-rooted connection to the Far East, where she has spent time over the years. Vibrant greens, lush textures and leafy canopies form the backdrop to her flourishing urban garden. The clever planting creates the feeling of being immersed in nature, whether in the English countryside or on another continent.

BELOW
The view from the top terrace includes Alison's favourite garden feature, the bird table. Filling this daily for the feeding visitors brings many different kinds of birds to the garden as well as the odd squirrel. Stopping to watch their activities provides the ideal opportunity to take a break from everyday tasks to simply observe and enjoy her surroundings.

Enjoyed from daybreak to the evening's end, the clever design allows for a flowing journey through differing areas. It feels like roaming through a story, chapter by chapter, enjoying all its unexpected twists and turns.

There is an initial courtyard behind the house – a suntrap with comfortable seating and Alison's own beautiful parasols for shade. The view opens out onto a series of falling terraces. There is a veranda to the side and a covered garden room before steps lead down to the first lawned enclosure, where cottage-garden planting gives way to lush shrubs. The bird table here is one of Alison's favourite features, offering many a moment to connect with the local wildlife and enjoy the sound of birdsong.

OPPOSITE
The garden room is an indoor-outdoor space that the family use all year round. Open to the view and sky thanks to its glazed walls and roof, the room is nonetheless cozy and warm even on the chilliest of days. It is the perfect vantage point from which to enjoy cloudless blue skies and crisp mornings in the winter without having to venture out into the cold.

LEFT

A freestanding sofa and a pair of matching armchairs create the feel of an outdoor living room. Arranged centrally in the garden, this area offers a clear view of both ends of the plot. The surrounding trees and shrubs muffle sound and provide shade, while the swaying boughs also bring natural movement.

RIGHT

Dainty wooden steps lead down to the final terrace. They blend beautifully with the chipped bark flooring. Chosen to evoke the idea of a forest floor, the woodchip softens the landscaping and absorbs noise. It is also an eco-friendly option – as the chips break down, they act as a mulch, adding nutrients to the soil and preventing weed growth while protecting plants from harsh weather.

"The garden is enjoyed by Alison and her family every day. Mornings start outside whatever the weather: the birds are fed, flowers dead headed and tea is taken."

Continuing down through the garden, further seating on the next level benefits from dappled light through the greenery. On the lowest and most secluded of the terraces, there is a dining area featuring a beautiful banquette seat sculpted into the stone levee. This grotto area feels most magical lit by flickering candles in the evening.

The garden is explored and enjoyed by Alison and her family every day. Mornings start outside whatever the weather: the birds are fed, flowers deadheaded and tea is taken. Then the space is used for relaxation, entertaining and even yoga, and the day ends with tucking up baby plants and watering everything before bedtime. The garden is dressed to make being outside comfortable and cozy at all times of year. Sumptuous throws and cushions, ample shades and rugs invite conversing, reading and resting. Old familiars mingle with new buys, and there are many sustainable solutions on display.

ABOVE

Overhanging ferns on the middle tier hide the private dining space below. Alison has added a parasol over the table for shelter and shading. Its trim mimics the fern fronds as they swirl in the breeze.

ABOVE RIGHT

Inherited from the previous owners, this sculptural bench carved into the embankment on the lowest terrace is made of stone slabs and rocks that have aged beautifully over time. It is a cool space to find peace and calm. Topped with cushions and padding to soften the stone, it is a very comfortable place to laze.

Attention has been paid to the next generation of gardeners in the family, too, as Alison has recently welcomed a granddaughter who loves to explore and find her feet. It is the simplest of shared skills, such as planting seeds and watching plants grow together, that make up quality hours spent at home with loved ones.

Wildlife is equally welcome in the garden thanks to carefully chosen houses and hotels for bugs and bees, as well as fragrant flowers that scent the air to entice winged insects. While the garden is well tended, Alison ensures that there are leaves left lying on the ground for hedgehogs to nestle and bundle into, damp spots for an array of amphibians and watering stations for all to use.

The garden is set to be enjoyed by all for years to come. Alison has worked hard to create this welcoming outdoor space for her family, but it is equally important to simply pause and take it all in, reflect and connect.

OPPOSITE

A vintage table and chairs live out their last years on the bottom terrace and are seen here dressed with low-key linens and candles. This area has been the setting for many a dinner and drinks party in the time that the family has lived here. It is a fantastic yet secluded space to escape to, located at the farthest end of the garden from the house. The canopy of trees keeps the terrace cool and also invites wildlife to flit between the leaves. This is the perfect place to hide away from it all.

SOURCES

FABRICS & TEXTILES

HUGATHOME
hugathome.co.uk
With a growing collection of natural and sustainable products, Phenox Textiles' online retail outlet Hug At Home sells rugs created from cotton, coir, bamboo, wool and recycled plastic.

KVADRAT
kvadrat.dk
This Danish company makes durable outdoor fabrics for upholstery, screens and more. The fabrics have a fluorocarbon-free water-repellent coating to keep them looking good.

PHIFER
phifer.com
Phifer's GeoBella outdoor fabrics are made of olefin, a 100% recyclable polypropylene textile. They are perfect for poolside comfort with designs suitable for cushions, upholstery and curtains.

THE STRIPES COMPANY
thestripescompany.com
This specialist company produces heavy-duty textiles inspired by our favourite outdoor seating. Offering replacement deckchair slings and cotton canvas by the metre in many styles, it also sells leftover remnants and patchwork squares for smaller upholstery and sewing projects.

SUNBRELLA
sunbrella.com
Sunbrella has a range of outdoor and marine textiles to suit all needs thanks to its pioneering weaving technology. The company uses recycled yarn within many of its fabrics.

WEAVER GREEN
weavergreen.com
This clever company creates all its rugs, cushions, baskets and blankets from recycled plastic bottles. Some items have the softness of wool yet in a water-resistant textile that is perfect for indoors or out.

SURFACES

CEMENT TILE SHOP
cementtileshop.com
Based in the US and shipping worldwide, this brand creates indoor and outdoor tiles using naturally sourced ingredients.

ECO OUTDOOR
ecooutdoorusa.com
Leading the market in natural and considered materials for outdoor surfaces, Eco Outdoor supplies wall cladding, flooring and tiles as well as tough and resilient garden furniture.

ECOSCAPE
ecoscapeuk.co.uk
Suitable for cladding and flooring, Ecoscape's wood-effect composite is made from reclaimed wood fibres and recycled plastic. The material is durable, easy to maintain and FSC certified.

GRANITECRETE
granitecrete.com
GraniteCrete is an innovative permeable landscaping surface suitable for pathways and drives. Unlike concrete, it enables water to drain through.

LASSCO
lassco.co.uk
A treasure trove of reclaimed home and garden wares, Lassco also has many different exterior surfaces and details to choose from, which will bring a unique finish to your garden.

MANDARIN STONE
mandarinstone.com
Mandarin Stone has a comprehensive collection of natural stone and porcelain outdoor tiles and cobbles. Ideal for long-term usage, stone is durable and allergy friendly.

MULTY HOME
multyhome.com
Bringing eco innovation to the garden, this company creates flooring, screens and outdoor accessories from recycled car tyres. Weather resistant and plant safe, its products are both durable and decorative.

FURNITURE, HEATING & LIGHTING

BIG GREEN EGG
biggreenegg.co.uk
Providing an eco-friendly outdoor cooking experience, this innovative ceramic barbecue oven is quick to heat and delivers the perfect temperature without burning excess fuel. Its design celebrates artisan crafts with a little help from space-age science.

DVELAS
dvelas.com
Reusing sailcloths from boats and yachts, this company upcycles the fabric into shades, seating and outdoor accessories. Each unique item is tagged with the details of its floating origins.

ECO FURN
ecofurn.eu
This Finnish brand makes outdoor furniture with sustainability and craft at the heart of every design. It uses FSC-certified Nordic timber and hemp rope, with any leftover wood and sawdust being repurposed to make heating briquettes.

ECO GRILL
ecogrill-uk.com
Made entirely from alder wood, Eco Grill's biodegradable single-use barbecue can grill, fry, boil or smoke food before burning away completely.

ENVIROBUILD
envirobuild.com
Envirobuild offers furniture and garden landscaping designs with a heart. Not only are all products part of a considered collection, 10% of all profits are donated to conservation charities such as the Rainforest Trust UK.

IRONFIRE
iron-fire.co.uk
This company's wide range of quality garden furniture and firepits combines unique designs, sustainability and affordability. It also provides spares and accessories so that you can update and repair its products over time.

MOBEK
mobek.co.uk
Mobek is a family-run business that makes and sells furniture constructed from recycled plastic with a woodgrain finish, from comfortable upholstered pieces to classic Adirondack chairs and rockers.

POTTERY BARN
potterybarn.com
Mindful of its carbon footprint, this US lifestyle store offers a range of sustainably sourced and artisan-made homewares.

PUJI
puji.com
Puji's beautiful furniture is designed to be used over many years, combining craftsmanship with graceful materials and superior design skills.

RH
rh.com
This design emporium sells artisan-crafted wares. Many of its outdoor furniture pieces are made from SVLK-certified Indonesian teak, which is sustainably grown and responsibly harvested, and a durable composite basket weave.

ROCKETT ST GEORGE
rockettstgeorge.co.uk
Offering furniture, lighting, parasols and accessories made from natural and upcycled materials, this company creates character-driven collections.

SCARAMANGA
scaramangashop.co.uk
Scaramanga is a wonderful source of vintage and upcycled furniture and accessories, which will bring a personalized look to your space.

SITTING SPIRITUALLY
sittingspiritually.co.uk
This firm's bespoke garden swings and swing seats are handcrafted to order using FSC-certified wood. A tree is planted for every seat sold.

SUSTAINABLE FURNITURE
sustainable-furniture.co.uk
Stocking wood and recycled plastic designs, this outdoor living emporium has a varied range that would suit many styles and budgets, from picnic tables and sunloungers to parasols and cushions.

TIKAMOON
tikamoon.co.uk
French brand Tikamoon creates contemporary furniture and fittings using natural materials and traditional woodworking methods. Each product has an 'eco note' rating based on six sustainability criteria.

WEST ELM
westelm.com
Producing modern yet timeless furniture and homewares, West Elm is proud of its indoor and outdoor collections made with FSC-certified timber.

HOMEWARE, WELLBEING & WILDLIFE

B&Q
diy.com
This emporium has its own sustainability program and is moving towards zero-waste, zero-carbon manufacturing. It also offers advice to help you create a greener garden.

CHALK & MOSS
chalkandmoss.com
Bringing biophilic design to the fore, this brand encourages us to connect with the outside world via the organic materials used in its pots, planters, shelving and potting-up tools.

DOBBIES
dobbies.com
A leading purveyor of garden equipment, Dobbies promotes peat-free gardening and offers more sustainable alternatives.

THE FUTURE KEPT
thefuturekept.com
This beautiful collection of ethically and sustainably made products includes copper gardening tools and outdoor incense. The company donates 1% of all sales to environmental not-for-profit groups.

GARDEN TRADING
gardentrading.co.uk
Garden Trading has a complete garden-room offering including sustainable and considered choices for furniture, lighting, heating and storage.

NATURAL COLLECTION
naturalcollection.com
As well as garden plants and pots, Natural Collection sells water butts, composters and solar-powered lighting, plus wildlife feeders and houses.

NKUKU
nkuku.com
This lifestyle store promotes handmade crafts and natural materials, offering a range of garden furniture and outdoor accessories made using recycled goods and waste materials.

NORDIC HOUSE
nordichouse.co.uk
A pioneer of slow living and craftsmanship, this company has sourced an elegant collection of outdoor firepits, cookers and candles to make your garden a magical place to spend the evening.

ORIGINAL ORGANICS
originalorganics.co.uk
The wildlife-welcoming garden accessories at Original Organics include feeders, baths, hotels and houses for bugs, birds and hedgehogs.

PROTECT THE PLANET
protecttheplanet.co.uk
This upcycled and eco-friendly lifestyle brand encourages buyers to enjoy the outdoors with natural wax candles, solar-powered lighting and grow-your-own inspiration.

PAINTS, STAINS & FINISHES

AURO
auropaint.co.uk
Auro's eco-friendly eggshell and gloss paints are natural and water based – the paint can even be composted if there are any leftovers.

GRAPHENSTONE
graphenstone.co.uk
With incredible eco credentials and impressive coverage, Graphenstone's paints are free from toxic substances and offer breathable outdoor coverage in multi-surface and lime finishes.

LAKELAND PAINTS
lakelandpaints.co.uk
Completely free from solvents, VOCs and other hazardous chemicals, Lakeland's masonry paint is an eco-friendly option available in 180 colours.

LICK
lickhome.com
Not only does Lick have a beautiful palette of outdoor paints, it also invests a portion of its profits in 4ocean's efforts to remove plastic from the ocean and in the One Tree Planted reforestation program.

ORGANOWOOD
organowood.com
Inspired by the ancient process of fossilization, this preservative uses organic catalysts to bind to wooden surfaces, making them look good naturally for longer.

OSMO
osmouk.com
Osmo uses purified and refined ingredients in its exterior wood finishes. These oils and waxes are suitable for use on fences, play equipment and furniture.

TREATEX
treatex.co.uk
With a range encompassing wood waxes, oils and colours as well as cleaning products and brushes, Treatex uses natural and sustainable ingredients. The brand's wildlife-friendly wood stains are ideal for bird boxes and beehives.

PICTURE CREDITS

KEY: a = above, b = below, r = right, l = left, c = centre

All photography by Dan Duchars

Endpapers The garden of Nyla Abraham and Paul Sadler of @_thesuburbancottagegarden_ in Bath; *1* The garden of Samantha Greetham, @cowparsley_and_foxgloves; *2* The garden of Nyla Abraham and Paul Sadler of @_thesuburban cottagegarden_ in Bath; *3l and c* The garden of Theresa Gromski in Birmingham, @theresa_gromski; *3r* The garden of Caroline and Rob Cowan of @wood_fired_garden and @offthewagon_ bar; *4* The garden of Alison and Neil Bosworth in Birmingham; *5ar* The garden of Julie Aldridge in Cambridgeshire, @aldridge julie; *5br* The garden of Abigail Ahern and Graham Scott in London, abigailahern.com; *6* The garden of Nyla Abraham and Paul Sadler of @_thesuburbancottagegarden_ in Bath; *7–8* The garden of Theresa Gromski in Birmingham, @theresa_gromski; *10* The garden of Kate Revere in Stoke Newington; *11ar* The garden of Alison and Neil Bosworth in Birmingham; *11cr* The garden of Isatu Chadborn of @life_of_isatu in Essex; *11br* The garden of Julie Aldridge in Cambridgeshire, @aldridgejulie; *12a* The garden of Isatu Chadborn of @life_of_isatu in Essex; *12b* The garden of Theresa Gromski in Birmingham, @theresa_ gromski; *13* The garden of Samantha Greetham, @cowparsley_ and_foxgloves; *14* The garden of Nyla Abraham and Paul Sadler of @_thesuburbancottagegarden_ in Bath; *15al* The London garden of Sarah Clark and Tom Lloyd; *15ar* The garden of Nyla Abraham and Paul Sadler of @_thesuburbancottagegarden_ in Bath; *15bl* The garden of Samantha Greetham, @cowparsley_ and_foxgloves; *15br* The garden of Abigail Ahern and Graham Scott in London, abigailahern.com; *16al* The garden of Abigail Ahern and Graham Scott in London, abigailahern.com; *16cl* The Yorkshire garden of Laura Stubbs, epitomestyling.co.uk, @laura_epitome_styling; *16bl* The garden of Alison and Neil Bosworth in Birmingham; *17* The garden of Theresa Gromski in Birmingham, @theresa_gromski; *18* The garden of Julie Aldridge in Cambridgeshire, @aldridgejulie; *19a and bl* The garden of Alison and Neil Bosworth in Birmingham; *19br* The garden of Theresa Gromski in Birmingham, @theresa_gromski; *20* The garden of Rasa T-Brasiene of @tiffyandflow in London; *21ar and br* The garden of Nyla Abraham and Paul Sadler of @_thesuburbancottagegarden_ in Bath; *21cr* The garden of Julie Aldridge in Cambridgeshire, @aldridgejulie; *22al* The garden of Isatu Chadborn of @life_of_isatu in Essex; *22ar* The garden of Julie Aldridge in Cambridgeshire, @aldridgejulie; *22bl* The garden of Alison and Neil Bosworth in Birmingham; *23* The garden of Kate Revere in Stoke Newington; *24* The garden of Abigail Ahern and Graham Scott in London, abigailahern. com; *25a and bl* The garden of Theresa Gromski in Birmingham, @theresa_gromski; *25br* The garden of Nyla Abraham and Paul Sadler of @_thesuburbancottagegarden_ in Bath; *26al* The garden of Julie Aldridge in Cambridgeshire, @aldridgejulie; *26bl* The garden of Theresa Gromski in Birmingham, @theresa_gromski; *26cl and 27* The garden of

Abigail Ahern and Graham Scott in London, abigailahern.com; *28–29* The garden of Julie Aldridge in Cambridgeshire, @aldridgejulie; *30al* The garden of Theresa Gromski in Birmingham, @theresa_gromski; *30br* The garden of Isatu Chadborn of @life_of_isatu in Essex; *31* The Cornish garden of Sharon Foskett, @blondies78; *32* The garden of Caroline and Rob Cowan of @wood_fired_garden and @offthewagon_bar; *33ar* The garden of Nyla Abraham and Paul Sadler of @_the suburbancottagegarden_ in Bath; *33cr* The Cornish garden of Sharon Foskett, @blondies78; *33br* The garden of Theresa Gromski in Birmingham, @theresa_gromski; *34al* The garden of Kay Prestney, @kinship_creativedc; *34ar and bl* The garden of Theresa Gromski in Birmingham, @theresa_gromski; *34br and 35* The garden of Julie Aldridge in Cambridgeshire, @aldridgejulie; *36* The garden of Theresa Gromski in Birmingham, @theresa_gromski; *37a* The garden of Rasa T-Brasiene of @tiffyandflow in London; *37b* The garden of Isatu Chadborn of @life_of_isatu in Essex; *38al* The garden of Alison and Neil Bosworth in Birmingham; *38cl and bl* The Cornish garden of Sharon Foskett, @blondies78; *39* The garden of Alison and Neil Bosworth in Birmingham; *40al* The garden of Julie Aldridge in Cambridgeshire, @aldridgejulie; *40ar and bl* The garden of Alison and Neil Bosworth in Birmingham; *40br* The Sussex garden of Julia Parker of @parkers_patch; *41al* The garden of Julie Aldridge in Cambridgeshire, @aldridgejulie; *41br* The Yorkshire garden of Linda Kilburn; *42* The garden of Nyla Abraham and Paul Sadler of @_thesuburbancottagegarden_ in Bath; *43al* The garden of Alison and Neil Bosworth in Birmingham; *43ar* The Sussex garden of Julia Parker of @parkers_patch; *43bl* The garden of Samantha Greetham, @cowparsley_and_foxgloves; *43br* The garden of Alison and Neil Bosworth in Birmingham; *44–45* The garden of Nyla Abraham and Paul Sadler of @_thesuburbancottagegarden_ in Bath; *46–57* The garden of Julie Aldridge in Cambridgeshire, @aldridgejulie; *58–65* The garden of Abigail Ahern and Graham Scott in London, abigailahern.com; *66–71* The Yorkshire garden of Linda Kilburn; *72–77* The Yorkshire garden of Laura Stubbs, epitomestyling.co.uk, @laura_epitome_styling; *78–85* The garden of Kate Revere in Stoke Newington; *86–95* The garden of Theresa Gromski in Birmingham, @theresa_gromski; *96–99* The London garden of Sarah Clark and Tom Lloyd; *100–105* The garden of Rasa T-Brasiene of @tiffyandflow in London; *106–115* The garden of Isatu Chadborn of @life_of_isatu in Essex; *116–125* The garden of Nyla Abraham and Paul Sadler of @_thesuburbancottagegarden_ in Bath; *126–131* The garden of Caroline and Rob Cowan of @wood_fired_garden and @offthe wagon_bar; *132–139* The Sussex garden of Julia Parker of @parkers_patch; *140–147* The garden of Kay Prestney, @kinship_creativedc; *148–155* The garden of Samantha Greetham, @cowparsley_and_foxgloves; *156–161* The Cornish garden of Sharon Foskett, @blondies78; *162–169* The garden of Alison and Neil Bosworth in Birmingham; *173ar* The garden of Isatu Chadborn of @life_of_isatu in Essex; *174* The garden of Alison and Neil Bosworth in Birmingham; *176* The garden of Abigail Ahern and Graham Scott in London, abigailahern.com.

BUSINESS CREDITS

ABIGAIL AHERN
12–14 Essex Road
London N1 8LN
T: +44 (0)20 7354 8181
E: customerservices@abigailahern.com
abigailahern.com
IG: @abigailahern
Pages 5br, 15br, 16al, 24, 26cl,
27, 58–65, 176.

ALISON BOSWORTH
thebalinesetradingcompany.com
IG: @thebalinesetradingcompany
Pages 4, 11ar, 16bl, 19a, 19bl, 22bl, 38al,
39, 40ar, 40bl, 43al, 43br, 162–169, 174.

ISATU CHADBORN
IG: @life_of_isatu
Pages 11cr, 12a, 22al, 30br, 37b, 106–115, 173.

JULIA PARKER
IG: @parkers_patch
Pages 40br, 43ar, 132–139.

JULIE ALDRIDGE
IG: @aldridgejulie
Pages 5ar, 11br, 18, 21cr, 22ar, 26al, 28–29,
34br, 35, 40al, 41al, 46–57.

KATE REVERE
Revere the Residence
150–152 Stoke Newington Church Street
London N16
revertheresidence.com
IG: @reveretheresidence
Pages 10, 23, 78–85.

KAY PRESTNEY
Kinship Creative Design Consultancy
@kinship_creativedc
Pages 34al, 140–147.

LAURA STUBBS
Epitome Styling
T: +44 (0)7791 365597
E: laura@epitomestyling.co.uk
epitomestyling.co.uk
IG: @laura_epitome_styling
Pages 16cl, 72–77.

LINDA KILBURN
Garden design by Stephen Bean
SBA Leisure Ltd – Leisure &
Landscape Designers
Malton
North Yorkshire YO17 8DB
T: +44 (0)1944 738017
sba-design.co.uk
Pages 41br, 66–71.

Boat house built by
Albert Thundercliffe
Grindale Woodworks Ltd
Mereside Barn Workshop
Grindale
Bridlington YO16 4XY
T: +44 (0)7803 189405
IG: @grindale_woodworks

Materials supplied by MKM
Building Supplies
T: +44 (0)1482 345678
E: hello@mkmbs.co.uk
mkmbs.co.uk
Pages 41br, 66–71.

NYLA ABRAHAM
IG: @_thesuburbancottagegarden_
Endpapers, 2, 6, 14, 15ar, 21ar, 21br,
25br, 33ar, 42, 44–45, 116–125.

RASA T-BRASIENE
IG: @tiffyandflow
Pages 20, 37a, 100–105.

ROB COWAN
Sussex-based mobile pub and
restaurant in a converted 1974 Bedford
TK horsebox, available for hire.
T: +44 (0)7764 466170
E: rob@offthewagon.pub
offthewagon.pub
IG: @offthewagon_bar

Bespoke ovens and outdoor kitchens
IG: @wood_fired_garden
Pages 3r, 32, 126–131.

SARAH CLARK
littlespree.com
IG: @littlespree

Garden design by Nicola Erskine-Tulloch
Pages 15al, 96–99.

SAMANTHA GREETHAM
IG: @cowparsley_and_foxgloves
Pages 1, 13, 15bl, 43bl, 148–155.

SHARON FOSKETT
IG: @blondies78
Pages 31, 33cr, 38cl, 38bl, 156–161.

THERESA GROMSKI
theresagromskistudio.com
IG: @theresa_gromski
Pages 3l, 3c, 7–8, 12b, 17, 19br, 25a, 25bl,
26bl, 30al, 33br, 34ar, 34bl, 36, 86–95.

INDEX

Page numbers in *italic* refer
to the illustrations

ACKNOWLEDGEMENTS

There are many people we would like to
thank in helping us create this book. First, a
huge credit must go to the wonderful team at
Ryland Peters & Small for taking us under their
wing once more. Their time, experience and
support are really appreciated.

We would also like to thank all the amazing owners
who invited us into their gardens and shared the stories
of how they created and nurtured their outdoor spaces.
Discovering how much their gardens mean to them is
a treasured memory and is something that resonates
wholeheartedly with us.

Thank you also to all our friends and followers who continue to
encourage us with your ideas and imaginations. We hope this book
inspires you as much as you do us. Please do continue to connect
with us and share your garden joys and growing tales. Find us on
Instagram and Facebook @thecontentednest #gardensforthesoul

Last but not least, we would like to thank our own families for the
unwavering compassion and kindness you have given us while we
were making this book. We look forward to spending much more
time in our own gardens with you. It is an opportunity to press pause,
watch the weather, see the seasons shift, nurture wildlife and ponder
our next project. Our gardens are a perfectly imperfect and soulful
place, in which we have the privilege to participate.

With love
Sara and Dan
The CONTENTed Nest